Financial Strategies For Selling A Farm Or Ranch

A Financial Guide For Saving Taxes On The Sale Of A Farm Or Ranch, Investing Sale Proceeds And Planning For Retirement

CHRIS NOLT

Financial Strategies For Selling A Farm Or Ranch

A Financial Guide For Saving Taxes On The Sale Of A Farm Or Ranch, Investing Sale Proceeds And Planning For Retirement

Copyright 2016 by Chris Nolt

All rights reserved. No part of this may be reproduced or transmitted in any manner whatsoever without written permission.

Limit of Liability / Disclaimer of Warranty: While the author has used their best efforts in preparing this book, they make no representations or warranties with respect to the accuracy and completeness of the contents of this book and specifically disclaim any warranties of merchantability for a particular purpose. No warranty may be created or extended by sales representatives or written sales material. The advice and strategies contained herin may not be suitable for your situation. You should consult with a professional where appropriate. Neither the publisher or the author shall be liable for any loss of profit or any other commercial damages, including but not limited to special, incidental, consequential or other damages.

www.solidrockproperty.com
www.solidrockwealth.com

Table of Contents

Introduction 1

Chapter 1 Ranch Sale Example 5

Chapter 2 Planning For The Sale Of Your Property 11

Chapter 3 IRC Section 1031 Exchange 27

Chapter 4 IRC Section 664 Charitable Remainder Trust 51

Chapter 5 Other Sale Planning Issues And Opportunities 81

Chapter 6 The Tax Reduction Wheel Of Fortune 97

Chapter 7 Investing Cash Proceeds From The Sale: Part One ... 109

Chapter 8 Investing Cash Proceeds From The Sale: Part Two ... 139

Chapter 9 Investing 1031 Exchange Sale Proceeds 181

Chapter 10 Retirement Planning Considerations 217

Conclusion 231

About The Author 233

Sources 235

Financial Strategies For Selling A Farm Or Ranch

Introduction

Having grown up working on ranches in central Montana and as a financial advisor to agricultural families for over 26 years, I understand how hard farmers and ranchers work for their money. I also understand the financial challenges and opportunities they face, especially in relation to selling their property and transitioning into retirement. Unfortunately, I've known agricultural families who have paid unnecessary taxes on the sale of their property and invested their money unwisely. Consequently, they were not able to enjoy the retirement lifestyle they had dreamed of and were unable to pass along the substantial amount of wealth to their heirs they had envisioned.

Without proper planning prior to the sale of a farm or ranch, the wealth a family has worked a lifetime to create may be eroded by

25% or more. Fortunately, financial tools exist that can help defer or avoid taxes on the sale of farm and ranch property. By utilizing the strategies discussed in this book, money that would go to paying taxes can instead be invested to generate income and provide an inheritance. To benefit from these tools, however, you must be proactive and engage in planning before a sale takes place.

Obtaining sound financial advice prior to selling a farm or ranch is critical. In my experience, however, farmers and ranchers are often reluctant to seek out financial assistance. Many are unwilling to pay the costs associated with tax and financial planning and some have a strong distrust of the financial services industry, often for good reason.

Farmers and ranchers are hardworking, industrious and self-reliant individuals. While these traits may have served these families well during the years of operating their business, this independent mindset can also damage them financially. Failing to plan with the right team of advisors may result in paying higher taxes and earning inferior investment returns.

I have a deep respect for agricultural families, and I am passionate about helping them make smart decisions with their money. That is one of the reasons I started my business. My companies are dedicated to helping families across the country save taxes on the sale of their farm or ranch and then helping them to invest their sale proceeds wisely.

I hope this book will be beneficial to you. If I can be of service to you, please call me at 406-582-1264.

Sincerely,

Chris Nolt, President
Solid Rock Wealth Management, Inc.
Solid Rock Realty Advisors, LLC.

CHAPTER 1

Ranch Sale Example

Many agricultural families face a dilemma today. On one hand, they know that selling their place is the smart thing to do. On the other hand, they have a hard time letting go of their land and the lifestyle they love. In addition, they do not want to pay the tax associated with a sale.

Here is an example of a family that faced these difficult decisions and how, through intelligent financial planning, they preserved their wealth and now enjoy a comfortable retirement. Perhaps you can relate to their story.

Ranch Sale Example

Bob and Mary, ages 67 and 65, owned a cattle ranch in central Montana. Their two children were grown, had their own careers and weren't interested in taking over the ranch. Bob and Mary deeply loved their ranch but had an increasing desire to travel and spend more time with their children and grandchildren. Bob's back pain was interfering more each year with his ability to operate the ranch and calving season was beginning to take a heavy toll on his mental and physical health. After much emotional deliberation, they decided it was time to sell.

Throughout the years of operating their ranch, profit from their operation went back into purchasing more land, cattle and equipment. When Bob and Mary listed their ranch for sale, the value of their home and ranch assets represented nearly 100% of their net worth. The value of their land had greatly increased and based on a tax projection from their CPA, Bob and Mary faced a tax bill of close to $900,000 if they were to cash out.

After several meetings and conference calls with their advisory team, Bob and Mary decided to utilize a 1031 Exchange and a Charitable Remainder Trust (CRT) to reduce the tax burden on the sale and to provide them with passive retirement income.

The ranch sold for $5.4 million. Bob and Mary did a 1031 exchange for $2 million into an office building leased to the Social Security Administration. This building offered a 10-year lease guaranteed by the full faith and credit of the U.S. federal government and generated a first year income, after all expenses, of $150,000. $1.5 million worth of land, cattle and equipment was sold through the CRT. Because the CRT is a tax-exempt entity, the proceeds sold in the CRT were not subject to tax. This money was invested in a diversified portfolio of mutual funds inside the CRT for the benefit of Bob and Mary. They chose an annual payout rate of 7% with the CRT, which provided them a first year income of $105,000.

Bob and Mary paid a small amount of tax on the remaining cash proceeds. This tax was largely reduced by the charitable deduction they received from transferring some of their property to the CRT. Bob and Mary were also able to withdraw tax-free money from the sale of their home through the Principal Residence Exclusion. By using the 1031 Exchange, Charitable Remainder Trust, Principal Residence Exclusion, and other tax saving strategies, Bob and Mary reduced their tax bill on the sale from approximately $900,000 to less than $50,000.

Bob and Mary used some of the cash proceeds to purchase a home in Montana and a second home in Arizona. Something they had long desired to do, but never had the cash or time for it, was to take their children and grandchildren to Disneyland. They used a small portion of the cash proceeds to take this long awaited trip. The remaining cash was invested in a conservative mutual fund portfolio. From this portfolio, they made annual withdrawals of $60,000.

From their annual income, Bob and Mary made annual gifts to a college savings plan for their grandchildren and purchased a $1 million second-to-die life insurance policy on their lives. The proceeds of this policy would ultimately pass income and estate tax-free to their children.

For the first time in their lives, Bob and Mary had the ability to travel for extended periods of time. They enjoyed an annual income that exceeded what they ever earned on the ranch and Bob didn't have to pull calves or feed cows in the wet, cold weather to earn it. Besides enjoying a comfortable retirement and providing a large inheritance for their children, Bob and Mary had the satisfaction of knowing their CRT would eventually provide a large sum of money to their church and favorite charity.

Annual Income	
Office building rent	$150,000
Charitable Remainder Trust payout	$105,000
Mutual fund portfolio distributions	$60,000
Total income	**$315,000**

CHAPTER 2

Planning For The Sale Of Your Property

Planning for the sale of your property and life afterwards should not begin when you have an interested buyer for your property. It should begin before even listing your property for sale. Too often, families wait until they have a signed contract before obtaining financial advice. Unfortunately, when this happens, it may be too late to utilize some tax-saving strategies.

Selling a farm or ranch can create significant tax consequences. However, there are financial tools and tax-saving strategies you can use to bypass these taxes. In the ranch sale example in chapter one, Bob and Mary took the best possible advantage of today's tax-saving tools and strategies, resulting in a savings of over $800,000. This enabled Bob and Mary to generate $50,000 of additional annual income and potentially leave a larger inheritance for their children and grandchildren.

If you sell your farm or ranch and do not utilize any tax-saving strategies, you will end up paying more in taxes. This means you will have less money left to invest. There are times when it is wise to take cash out of a sale for various reasons, but it is also prudent to explore tax-saving strategies with professional advisors before doing so.

Selecting The Right Tools For The Job

You utilize tools everyday on your farm and ranch. And you know exactly what tool to use to get a job done right. Just as there are tools for accomplishing tasks on a farm or ranch, there are financial tools for accomplishing financial objectives. To effectively utilize these tools, however, you need to consult with someone that has extensive training and experience in using them.

Two financial tools exist for saving taxes on the sale of appreciated property: the IRC Section 1031 Tax-Deferred Exchange and the IRC Section 664 Charitable Remainder Trust. These powerful tools allow you to preserve wealth and will be more thoroughly discussed in later chapters.

Tax Projection On The Sale

One of the first things I normally suggest to a family that is selling or considering selling property, is to get a tax projection on the sale from their CPA. This tax projection will determine if any tax-saving strategies should be considered. If there will be little to no taxes due on a sale, there is no need to utilize tax-saving strategies.

Team Approach

Effective planning for the sale of a farm or ranch often requires a team approach. You need a plan that takes into account tax, retirement, estate, investment planning and more. No single person has the expertise to effectively address each of these areas. That is why it is helpful to work with a team of advisors.

Your planning team may include the following:

- Farm and Ranch Real Estate Broker
- Certified Public Accountant
- Tax and Estate Planning Attorney
- Planned Giving Specialist
- Wealth Management Consultant/Registered Investment Advisor
- 1031 Exchange Intermediary
- Commercial Real Estate Agent
- Life Insurance Agent
- Real Estate Appraiser

A team of advisors collaborating together on your behalf helps maximize the effectiveness of your plan by making sure every item is properly addressed. Coordinating a team of professionals with expertise in each area can be a time-consuming task. A wealth management consultant who specializes in working with agricultural families selling their property can assist you with this difficult job.

Listing Your Property For Sale

Your farm or ranch likely represents the majority of your net worth. Choosing the right listing agent is a critically important decision. While you may be tempted to sell your property yourself, hiring a good farm and ranch broker can be well worth their commission. A good farm and ranch broker will not only help you obtain a top price for your property, but will facilitate a smoother transaction. They will aggressively market your property to the right group of buyers and head off potential issues in advance ... issues, that if not identified and dealt with in the beginning, could later end up costing you money and stress.

If you have a neighbor or someone else that is interested in purchasing your property, you may be able to avoid paying a real estate commission. In this case, it may still be wise to consult with a real estate attorney and a farm and ranch broker to make sure you receive the highest possible price and avoid making mistakes that could cost you later on down the line. Some brokers will help facilitate a sale for a set fee or hourly consulting charge in these cases.

It is important to work with a farm and ranch brokerage firm that specializes in farm and ranch sales. Selling a farm or ranch requires specific knowledge and expertise. You need someone who has a thorough understanding of water rights, mineral rights, environmental issues, land surveys, easements, building liability, Forest Service and BLM leases etc. They should also know how to properly assess the agricultural and recreational value as well as the value of your property's intrinsic aesthetic beauty. The person must be knowledgeable and conversant in all aspects of farm and ranch transactions.

A good real estate agent will help you use the most current and appropriate marketing methods to create desirability for your property. They will aggressively market the listing of your property with other real estate companies versus keeping the property to themselves in hopes of collecting both the listing and buyer side commission of the sale.

Two important things to look for when selecting a real estate agent are the person's experience and company track record. You want a company that is doing a large percentage of sales in the farm and ranch market and who has a reputation for honesty, integrity and professionalism. You want a company and agent who are well connected with the target audience for your property.

It is wise to interview several agents when considering the sale of your property. These agents will usually provide a free market analysis of your property and quote you a price they would list your property for. Be careful about listing your property with someone because they gave you the highest price. Some real estate agents will quote you a high price to get the listing. This may not be the best person to work with because listing your property too high in the beginning can end up costing you time and money and may ultimately have a negative impact on your bottom line.

One way to avoid this mistake is to have an appraisal of your property by a qualified appraiser prior to interviewing real estate agents. By knowing what your property is worth up front, you can base your decision of who to hire on factors besides price.

Only after you have selected the person to represent you on the sale of your property should you share this appraisal. A recent appraisal can be used as a great marketing tool for the person you list your property with. It will help speed up the process of a buyer securing financing as well as supporting the value placed on your property.

When you have chosen whom you are going to list your property with, be sure to carefully read the entire listing agreement prior to signing. If there is something you are uncertain or uncomfortable with, seek the advice of an attorney.

The questions below may serve as a useful tool in selecting the company and agent to sell your farm or ranch. If you would like names of reputable farm and ranch brokers, contact me at 406-582-1264.

Interview Guide For Selecting A Farm And Ranch Broker

1. Why should I hire you?
2. How long have you been a licensed real estate agent?
3. How long have you and your firm specialized in farm and ranch sales?
4. What percent of your sales are comprised of farm and ranch transactions?
5. What have you and your company's farm and ranch sales been over the last few years?

6. Explain how you value agricultural property?
7. Do you have experience in operating a farm or ranch?
8. Explain how you value recreational property?
9. What is your experience with recreational activities and properties?
10. What is your knowledge of water rights, mineral rights and land surveys?
11. How do you plan to market my property?
12. What publications do you plan to advertise my property in and how often?
13. What is your strategy for marketing my property on the internet?
14. How do you rank in search engines when buyers search for farm and ranch property for sale?
15. Will you be present for all property showings or will others be showing my property?
16. What has been the average percentage difference between what you have listed a property for and what it has sold for?
17. What has been the average length of time your listings have taken to sell?
18. How often will you communicate with me?
19. Do you limit the number of properties you list at any given time?
20. How many properties do you currently have listed and what is the total value of those listings?
21. Do you work by yourself or do you work with other agents within your company?
22. Do you aggressively market my property to other real estate companies?

23. Would you work with other real estate companies to sell my property or do you only work with "in-house" buyers so you do not have to split your commission?
24. Do you represent me exclusively or are you a dual agent representing prospective buyers too?
25. How would you determine the right price for my property should I choose to list with you?
26. Do you have any suggestions on what I could do to increase the value of my property?
27. What do you perceive as the biggest challenge in selling my property and what could be done to effectively deal with that challenge?
28. If I were to hire you, what can I do to assist you in selling my property?
29. What do you see happening to the prices of properties like mine over the next few years and what are your reasons for that?
30. Do you have experience in selling farm or ranch property in a Charitable Remainder Trust?
31. What commission do you charge and is this negotiable?
32. If a buyer approaches me directly, would you reduce your commission?
33. Do you offer a reduced commission on personal property that I include with the sale of my land?
34. How long is your typical listing agreement for?
35. Are there any obligations to you once that listing expires?
36. Can you provide me with names and contact information of some of your clients?

Taxation Of Farm And Ranch Assets

Various tax rates and tax treatment apply to the different types of assets involved with the sale of a farm or ranch. It is imperative that you seek direction from your tax advisors when purchase price allocation is being negotiated.

Allocation Of Sales Price

How you allocate the sales price to the assets of your ranch will determine the tax you may ultimately pay. Conflict can arise when negotiating how to allocate the sales price. You, the seller, want to pay tax at the capital gain rate because it is currently lower than ordinary income tax rates. Conversely, the buyer will want to allocate more of the sale price to depreciable assets.

When a farm or ranch is purchased or sold, both the buyer and seller must report to the IRS the allocation of sales price. IRS form 8594 is titled the Asset Acquisition Statement. This form should also be attached to the buyer and seller's federal income tax return for the year of the sale.

Below Is A List Of Asset Categories And The Type Of Tax Owed On Each Category

Inventory and Supplies: Crops, fertilizer, etc.
- Taxed at ordinary income rates

Livestock
- Raised livestock – breeding stock
    - Cattle and horses – held more than two years – taxed at capital gain rates

- Other livestock – held more than one year – taxed at capital gain rates
- There is no cost basis in raised livestock
- Purchased livestock – Breeding stock
    - Cattle and horses – held more than 2 years – taxed at capital gain rates
    - Other livestock – held more than 1 year – taxed at capital gain rates
    - Cost basis is purchase price. Depreciation recapture rules apply
- Purchased or raised livestock that is held for sale
    - Taxed at ordinary income rates

Equipment
- Irrigation systems, swathers, bailers, tractors, etc. IRC Section 1245 assets. Recapture of depreciation applies.

Ranch House
- IRC Section 121 Exclusion:
- Gain does not apply to extent of any depreciation claimed after 5/6/97. IRC Section 121 (d) (6).
- No allocation of exclusion is required if both the residential and business portions of the property are with the same dwelling unit, other than to the extent the gain is attributable to depreciation after 5/6/97.
- 121 Exclusion is not eligible for homes owned in a corporation.

Buildings
- Single-Use Property – IRC Section 1245 depreciation recapture applies.
- IRC Section 1250 Property – potential depreciation recapture may apply.

Land
- Gain taxed at capital gain rates

Below Is A Summary Of The Five Ways Investors May Be Taxed On The Sale Of A Farm Or Ranch:

1. **Federal Ordinary Income Tax:** Taxpayers will be taxed at rates up to 39.6% depending on taxable income.

2. **Federal Capital Gain Taxes:** Investors owe Federal capital gain taxes on the their economic gain depending upon their taxable income. Since a new higher capital gain tax rate of 20% has been added to the tax code, investors exceeding the $400,000 taxable income threshold for single filers and married couples filing jointly with over $450,000 in taxable income will be subject to the new higher tax rate. The previous Federal capital gain tax rate of 15% remains for investors below these threshold income amounts.

3. **State Taxes:** Taxpayers must also take into account the applicable state tax, if any, to determine their total tax owed. Some states have no state taxes at all, while other states, like California, have a 13.3% top tax rate. Montana currently has a top rate of 6.9%.

4. **Depreciation Recapture:** Depreciation recapture is the IRS procedure for collecting income tax on a gain realized by a taxpayer when they dispose of an asset that had previously provided an offset to ordinary income for the taxpayer through depreciation. Taxpayers will be taxed at a rate of 25% on all depreciation recapture.

5. **New Medicare Surtax Pursuant to IRC Section 1411:** The Health Care and Education Reconciliation Act of 2010 added a new 3.8% Medicare Surtax on "net investment income." This 3.8% Medicare surtax applies to taxpayers with "net

investment income" who exceed threshold income amounts of $200,000 for single filers and $250,000 for married couples filing jointly. Pursuant to IRC Section 1411, "net investment income" includes interest, dividends, capital gains, retirement income and income from partnerships (as well as other forms of "unearned income").

2016 Federal Capital Gain Tax Rates				
Single Taxpayer	Married Filing Jointly	Capital Gain Tax Rate	Section 141 Medicare Surtax*	Combined Tax Rate
$0 - $36,250	$0 - $72,500	0%	0%	0%
$36,250 - $200,000	$72,500 - $250,000	15%	0%	15%
$200,000 - $400,000	$250,000 - $450,000	15%	3.80%	18.80%
$400,001+	$450,001+	20%	3.80%	23.80%

*The 3.8% Medicare surtax only applies to "net investment income" as defined in IRC §1411.

Medicare Surtax Tax On Net Investment Income

The sale of ranch property may or may not be subject to the 3.8% surtax on net investment income. The rules and methods for computing this tax are complex and beyond the scope of this book. If you are considering selling property, make sure to seek the guidance of your CPA in determining if you will have to pay this tax.

There are other exceptions, but generally whether or not you will be subject to the 3.8% tax on net investment income depends on whether the gain is attributable to an active business of the entity and whether the taxpayer materially participates in that business.

Generally, a passive activity is one in which the taxpayer does not "materially participate". IRC section 469 (h)(1) defines "material participation" as involvement in the operation of the activity on a regular, continuous, and substantial basis.

Here are a couple of examples of situations where the taxpayer would be subject to the 3.8% tax on net investment income.

Example 1:

Two siblings own a farm; one runs it and the other is a passive investor. The sibling actively working on the property will generally not be subject to the tax on sale of the farm, but the gain on the sale realized by the passive sibling would (to the extent he and his spouse's income exceeds $250,000) be taxed.

Example 2:

If you own property but lease it out, you will likely be subject to the tax.

The good news is that the 3.8% tax on net investment income can be deferred by selling the property through a 1031 exchange or CRT.

Summary

Without proper planning prior to a sale of a farm, or ranch, the wealth a family has worked for a lifetime to create can be eroded by up to 25% or more.

Effective planning for the sale often requires a team approach. You need a plan that takes into account tax, retirement, estate, investment planning and more. No single person has the expertise to effectively address each of these areas. That is why it's helpful to work with a team of advisors.

Hiring a professional farm and ranch broker can help you obtain top dollar for your property and can facilitate a successful sale. Selling a farm or ranch requires specific knowledge and expertise. Selecting the right company and person to sell your property is very important.

Various tax rates and tax treatments apply to the different types of assets involved with the sale of a farm or ranch. How you allocate the sales price to the assets of your ranch will determine the tax you may ultimately pay. It is imperative that you seek direction from your tax advisors when purchase price allocation is being negotiated.

CHAPTER 3

IRC Section 1031 Exchange

The IRC Section 1031 Exchange is one of the most powerful tax-saving and wealth-building tools available for people selling highly appreciated (or depreciated) real estate. A properly structured 1031 exchange allows a family selling a farm or ranch to sell land, to reinvest the proceeds in other real estate, and to defer capital gain taxes.

To quote the tax code, IRC Section 1031 (a)(1) states: "No gain or loss shall be recognized on the exchange of property held for productive use in a trade or business or for investment, if such property is exchanged solely for property of like-kind which is to be held either for productive use in a trade or business or for investment."

Many farmers and ranchers believe the "like-kind" definition means they have to exchange their land into other land. This is not the case. Fortunately, the definition for "like-kind" property is very broad. One can exchange land into other types of investment property.

Benefits Of A 1031 Exchange

There are many potential benefits for a property owner who successfully executes a 1031 exchange. Some of these include:

1. Tax Deferral (Immediate And Indefinite)

In a properly executed 1031 exchange, capital gain taxes are deferred and transferred to "replacement property". Taxes are not due until the taxpayer sells the "replacement property" without utilizing a 1031 exchange or CRT. Since there is no limit to the number of exchanges a property owner can complete, it is possible to defer the payment of tax indefinitely.

The 1031 exchange is commonly referred to as a tax "deferred" exchange, implying that taxes are not eliminated, only deferred until the replacement property is later sold in a taxable transaction. However, it is possible to potentially eliminate capital gain taxes altogether on the sale of property by exchanging into and holding property until death. Under current tax law, heirs of a descendant's property receive a "step-up" in basis of the property's tax basis to its fair market value upon death. This "step-up" in basis could conceivably enable the heirs to inherit property and then sell the property for fair market value soon after the decedent's death and pay little or no tax. Thus, by employing the 1031 exchange until death, it may be possible to not only defer taxes on the sale of property, but to permanently eliminate them. This is why we often advise our clients to swap until they drop.

2. Improvement In Cash Flow Return

A typical farm or ranch has a very low cash flow return based on the value of the property. By selling farm and ranch land and exchanging into other types of commercial real estate, you may be able to greatly increase your annual cash flow rate of return.

3. Consolidation Or Diversification

Families selling a farm or ranch have the ability to consolidate large tracts of land into one or more properties. As a risk reduction strategy, you may choose to exchange into different types of properties in different geographic locations.

4. Elimination Of Active Management Of The Investment

Operating a farm or ranch involves a lot of hard work. Exchanging farm and ranch land into other passive real estate investments or into properties that are professionally managed, may enable you to free yourselves of the day-to-day activities of running your farm or ranch. Ironically, an agricultural family can often sell their place and increase their income without having to work nearly as hard for it.

5. Wealth Building

The greatest potential benefit from using a 1031 exchange may be the ability to preserve all of the equity in the property you are selling. Deferring taxes on a sale allows the seller to reinvest the full sales proceeds, undiluted by tax. The ability to invest money that would have gone to taxes in additional real estate may enable you to generate more income for retirement and pass more wealth to your children and grandchildren.

Consider the following example: A married couple sells land for $5 million with a cost basis of $1 million. Assuming a combined federal and state capital gain tax rate of 25%, they would pay approximately $1,000,000 in taxes if they were to cash out.

If this same couple were to do a 1031 exchange on the full $5 million sale, this $1,000,000 that would have gone to pay taxes could be invested in additional real estate. Assuming this real estate returned 7% per year, it would generate an additional $70,000 per year of income.

Not only would this couple benefit from the additional income the real estate generates while they are alive, if they hold the property until they die and if real estate continues to receive a step up in basis upon death, they could potentially pass several million dollars more to their heirs and their heirs may avoid the capital gain taxes on the property entirely!

Types Of Exchanges

There are several different types of exchanges. The most common is the delayed exchange. While most of our discussion will be devoted to the delayed exchange, below is a brief explanation of each type of exchange.

Before describing the types of exchanges, it will be helpful for you to understand the terms "relinquished property" and "replacement property". Relinquished property is the term given to property sold in a 1031 exchange. Replacement property is the term given to property one is exchanging into.

1. Delayed Exchange

A Delayed Exchange is an exchange in which the replacement property is acquired at a later date than the closing of the sale of the relinquished property. The exchange is not simultaneous or on the same day. This type of exchange is sometimes referred to as a "Starker Exchange" after the well known Supreme Court case which ruled in favor of the taxpayer who filed suit against the IRS before the Internal Revenue Code provided regulations for delayed exchanges. There are strict time frames for completing a qualified delayed exchange. These time frames will be discussed later in this chapter.

2. A Simultaneous Exchange

A Simultaneous Exchange is an exchange in which the closing of the relinquished property and the replacement property occur on the same day, usually back to back. There is no interval of time between the two closings. This type of exchange often happens with farm and ranch property where two neighbors wish to trade property.

3. A Reverse Exchange

A Reverse Exchange (sometimes referred to as a "parking arrangement") is an exchange in which the replacement property is purchased and closed on before the relinquished property is sold. Usually, an Exchange Accommodation Titleholder (EAT) takes title to the replacement property and holds title until the taxpayer can find a buyer for the relinquished property. Subsequent to the closing of the relinquished property, the EAT conveys title to the replacement property to the taxpayer to close out the taxpayer's forward exchange.

4. Build To Suit Exchange

The Build-To-Suit exchange, also referred to as a "Construction or Improvement Exchange", is an exchange in which a taxpayer desires to acquire a property and arrange for construction of improvements on the property before it is received as replacement property. This type of exchange gives the taxpayer performing the exchange the opportunity to use all or part of the exchange funds for construction, renovations or new improvements to the replacement property. In this type of transaction, the taxpayer will contract with an Exchange Accommodation Titleholder (EAT), similar to the reverse exchange described above, to construct the improvements within the exchange period and then convey the improved property to the taxpayer.

The Role Of A Qualified Intermediary

A 1031 Exchange Qualified Intermediary (QI), also known as an Accommodator or Facilitator, is a company that is in the business of facilitating 1031 exchanges. In most cases, the use of a QI is essential to the completion of a valid delayed exchange.

When performing a 1031 exchange, a QI enters into a written agreement with the taxpayer. A QI acquires the right to sell the relinquished property on behalf of the taxpayer, completes the transfers of the relinquished property, acquires the right to close on the replacement property and completes the transfers of the replacement property to the taxpayer pursuant to the Exchange Agreement. The QI holds the proceeds from the sale of the relinquished property in a trust or escrow account in order to ensure the taxpayer never has actual or "constructive receipt" of the sale proceeds.

Anyone who is related to the taxpayer, or who has had a financial relationship with the taxpayer (aside from providing routine financial services) within the two years prior to the close of escrow of the exchange cannot serve as the QI. This means that the taxpayer cannot use his or her own CPA, attorney or real estate agent to complete the exchange. A QI should be bonded and insured against errors and omissions and should utilize safe banking services for the protection of the exchange funds.

If you would like a list of Qualified Intermediaries with experience in performing 1031 exchanges on the sale of a farm or ranch, contact our office at 406-582-1264.

Basic Rules For A 1031 Exchange

1. Relinquished Property Must Be Qualifying Property

Qualifying property is property held for investment purposes or used in a taxpayer's trade or business. Investment property includes real estate held for investment or income producing purposes. Property used in a farm or ranch includes livestock, machinery and equipment. While the rules for "like-kind" real estate are fairly broad, the rules for exchanging other types of property are less flexible. While it is possible to perform an exchange on the sale of livestock and equipment and other types of personal property, the equipment must be exchanged for like-class equipment and the livestock must be exchanged for like-class livestock. For example, bulls must be exchanged for bulls, cows for cows and horses for horses. Saving taxes on the sale of livestock and equipment is often achieved through the use of a Charitable Remainder Trust. This will be discussed in the next chapter.

Property that does not qualify for a 1031 exchange includes:

- A principal residence
- Land under development for resale
- Construction or fix and flip properties for resale
- Property purchased or held for resale
- Inventory property
- Stocks, bonds or notes
- LLC membership interests
- Partnership interests

2. Replacement Property Must Be Like Kind

Replacement property in a 1031 exchange must be "like-kind" to the relinquished property.

A common misconception among many farmers and ranchers is that they must exchange their land into other land. This is not true. Fortunately, the definition for "like-kind" real estate given by the Internal Revenue Code is very broad. Qualifying replacement property can be virtually any real property that will be held by the taxpayer for investment purposes or used in a trade or business. Land can be exchanged for other types of property such as an office building, retail store, industrial warehouse, apartment complex etc.

3. Replacement Property Title Must Be In The Same Name As The Relinquished Property

One must take title to replacement property in the same way they held title in the relinquished property. For example, if a husband and wife own property in joint tenancy, replacement property must be deeded to both spouses in the same manner. Similarly, corporations, partnerships, limited liability companies or trusts must be on the title of the replacement property the same as they were on the relinquished property.

4. Any Boot Received In Addition To Like-Kind Replacement Property Will Be Taxable (to the extent of gain realized on the exchange)

The term "boot" refers to any property received in an exchange that is not considered "like-kind." Cash boot refers to the receipt of cash. Mortgage boot (also called "debt relief") is a term describing an exchanger's reduction in mortgage liabilities on a replacement property. Any personal property received is also considered boot in a real property exchange transaction.

A taxpayer must not receive "boot" from an exchange in order for the exchange to be completely tax deferred. Any boot received from the exchange is taxable to the extent of gain realized on the exchange.

Boot received can result from a variety of factors. Two of the most common of these result from "trading down" in a 1031 exchange. Trading down occurs when the replacement property is not of equal or greater value than the relinquished property. For example, if a taxpayer takes cash out of the exchange, or does not acquire a comparable amount of debt on his replacement property as he had on his relinquished property, he will end up trading down because there is not enough cash and/or debt to purchase a replacement property of value equal to his relinquished property.

In summary, if a taxpayer wishes to fully defer tax on an exchange, they must meet two requirements:

1. Reinvest the entire net proceeds in one or more replacement properties.
2. Acquire one or more replacement properties with the same or greater amount of debt. An exception to this requirement is that a taxpayer performing an exchange can offset a reduction in debt by adding cash to the replacement property at closing.

A good way to remember this is to understand that for a taxpayer to defer 100% of the tax in an exchange, they must "trade up or stay equal in debt and equity".

The "Held For" Requirement

To qualify for a 1031 exchange, the relinquished property and the replacement property must both have been acquired and "held for" investment or for use in a trade or business. The amount of time that the property must be "held for" is not clearly defined in the Internal Revenue Code.

The position of the IRS has been that if a taxpayer's property was acquired immediately before an exchange, or if the replacement property is disposed of immediately after an exchange, it was not held for the required purpose and the "held for" requirement was not met. This is typically not an issue with farm and ranch sales since the property has generally been owned for many years.

Since there is no safe harbor holding period for complying with the "held for" requirement, the IRS interprets compliance based on their view of the taxpayer's intent. Intent is demonstrated by facts and circumstances surrounding the taxpayer's acquisition of ownership of the property and what the taxpayer does with the property.

Partial Exchanges

Some people mistakenly think that in order to perform a 1031 exchange, they must exchange 100% of their sale proceeds. This is not true. It is possible to perform a partial exchange. Performing a partial exchange is often desirable because it may enable a family to pay off debt, diversify their sales proceeds into other investments and provide cash for liquidity purposes. A partial 1031 exchange can also be combined with a Charitable Remainder Trust and a cash sale as part of a comprehensive tax saving and retirement income plan. To see an example of how a 1031 exchange is combined with a CRT on the sale of a highly appreciated ranch, see chapter six.

Time Restrictions

There are strict time frames pertaining to the identification and receipt of the replacement property for the completion of a delayed exchange.

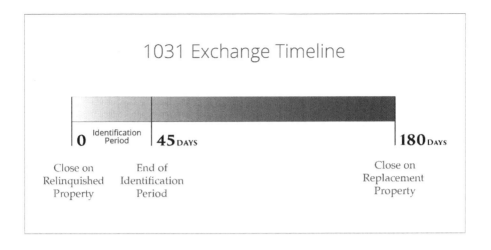

1. **45-Day Rule For Identification:** The first time restriction for a delayed exchange is for the taxpayer to either close on the purchase of the replacement property or to identify the potential replacement property(ies) within 45 days from the date of transfer of the relinquished property. The identification notice must be by written document (the Identification Notice) signed by the taxpayer and received by the Qualified Intermediary by midnight of the 45th day. After 45 days have expired, it is not possible to close on any property which was not identified in the 45-day letter. Failure to submit the 45-Day Letter causes the Exchange Agreement to terminate and the QI will disburse all unused funds in their possession to the taxpayer.

Property Identification Rules

The numbers of potential replacement properties identified are subject to the following rules:

- **Three Property Rule:** Any three properties regardless of their market value.
- **200% Rule:** Any number of properties as long as the aggregate

fair market value of the replacement properties does not exceed 200% of the value of the relinquished property.

- **95% Rule:** Any number of properties if the fair market value of the properties actually received by the end of the exchange period is at least 95% of the aggregate fair market value of all the potential replacement properties identified.

2. 180-Day Rule For Receipt Of Replacement Property: The Replacement Property must be received and the exchange completed no later than:

- 180 days after the transfer of the relinquished property or
- The due date of the taxpayer's income tax return, including extensions, for the tax year in which the relinquished property was transferred.

There is no provision for extension of the 180 days for any circumstance or hardship. There are provisions for extensions for presidentially declared disaster areas.

If an exchange takes place late in a tax year, the 180 day deadline can be later than the April 15 filing date of the tax return. If the exchange is not complete by the filing date, the return must be put on extension to properly extend the deadline for the full 180 days. Failure to put the return on extension can cause the replacement period for the exchange to end on the due date of the return.

Summary Of The Delayed Exchange Process

Here is a summary of the 1031 delayed exchange process:

1. The taxpayer arranges for the sale of their relinquished property.
2. At closing, sales proceeds go to a Qualified Intermediary.
3. The taxpayer identifies, in writing, potential replacement properties within 45 days of closing on the relinquished property.
4. The taxpayer closes on the replacement property(ies) and completes the exchange within 180 days of closing on the sale of the relinquished property.

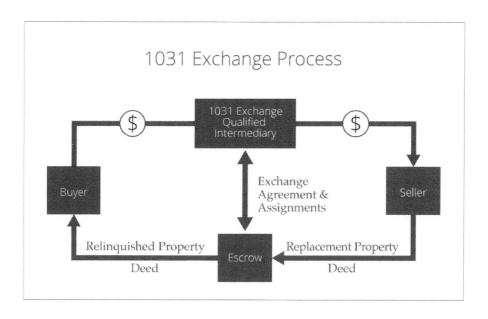

Related Party Exchanges

Special rules apply to exchanges involving related parties. Here are rules involving three different scenarios:

Exchange Of Property Between Related Parties

There is a special rule for exchanges between related parties which requires related taxpayers exchanging property with each other to hold the exchanged property for at least two years following the exchange to qualify for non-recognition of gain treatment. If either party disposes of the property received in the exchange and effects a shift in the cost basis of the property before the end of the two-year period, any gain or loss that would have been recognized on the original exchange must be taken into account on the date that the disqualifying disposition occurs.

Sale To An Unrelated Party, Replacement Property From A Related Party

A taxpayer will often desire to sell to an unrelated party and receive replacement property from a related party. According to the IRS, this type of related party transaction doesn't work if the related party receives cash. However, if the related party is also doing an exchange (and is not "cashing out") then it is okay to receive replacement property from a related party.

Sale To A Related Party, Replacement From An Unrelated Party

A taxpayer will often sell to a related party but receive replacement property from an unrelated party. This is okay but it has been unclear whether the related party was required to hold the property it acquired from the taxpayer for two years.

The rules defining who is considered a related party are broad. Make sure to speak with a Qualified Intermediary to be sure your exchange will not be disqualified because of these rules.

Multiple-Asset Exchanges

In addition to the sale of land, a farm or ranch sale often involves the sale of a principal residence, machinery, equipment and livestock. Machinery, equipment and livestock are eligible for an exchange but the exchange rules are more restrictive for these assets.

The U.S. Treasury Department has issued regulations that govern how multiple-asset exchanges such as these are to be reported. The regulations establish "exchange groups" which are separately analyzed for compliance with the like-kind replacement property requirements and rules for boot.

The Multiple-Asset regulations are complex and require the services of a tax professional for analysis purposes and income tax reporting. The tax professional is essential for helping to determine values and allocations of sale and purchase price.

A charitable remainder trust can be used to avoid tax on the sale of livestock, machinery and equipment. This will be discussed in chapter four.

Principal Residences

A principal residence is the home that you physically occupied and personally used the most during the five years preceding the sale of your property. When a home is involved with the sale of a farm or ranch, it is common for the closing of the relinquished property to be divided into two separate closings; one for the home and one for the rest of the property. The proceeds applicable to the sale of the home are usually disbursed to the taxpayer and not retained by the QI in the exchange escrow. The balance of the proceeds is retained by the QI for use in acquiring like-kind replacement property under the exchange agreement.

Exchanges that include personal property of significant value should reference the personal property in the exchange agreement and be completed in a manner that complies with all of the exchange rules concerning identification.

Vacation Homes

Most tax and exchange professionals agree that a vacation home can qualify for a 1031 exchange if the vacation home is also used for rental purposes. For example, if a vacation home is used less than 14 days per year for personal use then the personal use is disregarded and the home is considered investment property. Likewise, the taxpayer may use the home for up to 30 days per year for personal use if the home is rented out for the remaining 11 months. In this event, the home is still considered held for investment purposes and eligible for an exchange. Obviously, if the home is used 100% for personal use, then it does not qualify for an exchange.

In summary, in order for a vacation home to qualify 100% for a 1031 exchange, the taxpayer's personal use of the property must be less than the greater of 15 days, or 10% of the number of days during the year for which the dwelling is rented (at market value rents).

Personal use includes use by family members of the taxpayer's family. It does not, however, include bona fide work-days a taxpayer is at the residence. The taxpayer should consult with their CPA to ensure they are compliant.

If a vacation home is used partly for personal use and partly for investment purposes but is never rented out, things become more complicated. If the personal use is merely incidental, part of the property may still be eligible for an exchange. In order for a vacation home to qualify 100% for a 1031 exchange, the taxpayer's personal use of the property must be less than the greater of 15 days, or 10% of the number of days during the year for which the dwelling is rented (at market value rents).

Water, Timber And Mineral Rights

Water, timber and mineral rights may also be eligible for exchange. In many states, water rights are treated as real property interests. In those states where water rights are classified as real property interests, the conveyance or long term leasing of water rights could be utilized for the purposes of effecting a 1031 exchange into other "like kind" investment property.

With regard to timber rights, there have been an increasing number of farmers and ranchers who own timber property and entered into timber sale contracts with various logging companies. They have attempted to use those sale proceeds to acquire properties in a section 1031 exchange. Unfortunately, the Internal Revenue Service has relied upon a 1953 tax court case, known as the Oregon Lumber Company Case, in disallowing those transactions as exchanges.

Timber rights, however, much like water rights or mineral rights, are classified as real property interests in many states. Properly structured, the conveyance of timber rights should be the basis for an exchange into other "like kind" property.

An exchange of real estate for mineral rights is permitted if the mineral rights relinquished or acquired in an exchange constitute an interest in real property that is "like-kind" to a fee interest in real estate under federal tax law. The determination of whether a mineral right will be considered like-kind to a fee interest in real estate depends on: the specific nature of the rights granted under the mineral contract, the duration of those rights, and whether the law of the state in which the mineral interests are located would characterize the mineral rights as an interest in real property rather than an interest in personal property.

For example, a "production payment" is considered personal property because it is a bare right to receive income rather than an ownership interest in the minerals comprising the underlying real property. On the other hand, a royalty is considered "like-kind" real property and can be exchanged for any other real property. The primary distinction between these two interests is the term of the respective interest. In the case of a royalty interest, the royalty continues until the oil or gas deposit is exhausted. A production payment usually terminates when a specified quantity of oil or gas has been produced or a stated amount of proceeds have been received.

Easements

Although it is important to look to the treatment of easements under the applicable state laws, in many cases an easement is considered like-kind to any other like-kind real property held for productive use in a trade or business or for investment.

The following are qualified exchanges:

- An agricultural conservation easement in perpetuity in a farm found to be real property, for a fee simple interest in real property.
- An exchange of agricultural easements over two farms for fee-simple title in a different farm.
- A perpetual conservation easement encumbering real property for the fee simple interest in either farm land, ranch land, or commercial real property.
- A scenic conservation easement, found to be real property under state law, for a fee simple interest in timber, farm land, or ranch land.

Unharvested Crops

Depending upon state law, un-harvested crops may be considered real property. If so, then it is wise to exchange the farmland before harvest. Harvested crops are not eligible for a 1031 exchange given they are considered inventory and taxable as ordinary income unless the presence of a 30-year lease for the farmland exists.

Purchase And Sale Agreement Language

Purchase and sale agreements should indicate the taxpayer's intent to perform a 1031 exchange, as well as call for cooperation from the parties to the transaction. Here is some sample language:

Language For "Relinquished Property" Contract

"Buyer herein acknowledges that it is the intention of the seller to complete an IRC section 1031 tax-deferred exchange. Buyer agrees the seller's rights and obligations under this agreement may be assigned for the purpose of completing such exchange and this agreement is part of an integrated, interdependent exchange agreement. Buyer agrees to cooperate with the seller in any manner necessary to enable seller to qualify for and complete said exchange at no additional cost or liability to buyer."

Language For "Replacement Property" Contract

"Seller herein acknowledges that it is the intention of the buyer to complete an IRC section 1031 tax-deferred exchange. Seller agrees the buyer's rights and obligations under this agreement may be assigned for the purpose of completing such exchange and this agreement is part of an integrated, interdependent exchange agreement. Seller agrees to cooperate with the buyer in any manner necessary in order to qualify for and complete said exchange at no additional cost or liability to seller".

Summary

The IRC section 1031 exchange can be a powerful tool for saving taxes and building wealth. A 1031 exchange does not avoid tax, it only defers the tax. However, by holding exchanged property until death, one's heirs may inherit property with a "stepped-up" basis upon death, conceivably allowing them to sell property and avoid capital gain taxes altogether.

The 1031 exchange offers several tax and wealth building benefits.

When considering a 1031 exchange, do not let the tax benefits override the replacement property investment decision. In other words, don't let the tax tail wave the investment dog. A 1031 exchange should only be performed if there is suitable property to exchange into. This is one reason why it is important to be proactive when planning for a sale.

There are strict time parameters involved with a 1031 exchange. Replacement property must be identified in writing within 45 days of closing on the sale of the relinquished property and the replacement property must be closed on within 180 days of the closing of the relinquished property.

There are many types of exchanges and many requirements that need to be satisfied for completing a successful exchange. A Qualified Intermediary is in the business of facilitating 1031 exchanges. If you are considering a 1031 exchange, be sure to consult with a reputable tax professional and Qualified Intermediary that have extensive experience with farm and ranch exchanges.

CHAPTER 4

The Charitable Remainder Trust

A Charitable Remainder Trust (CRT) is one of the most powerful financial tools available for families selling a farm or ranch. It enables a family selling appreciated property to bypass tax on the sale and generate lifetime income for retirement. Not only can you bypass tax on the sale of land with a CRT, you can also bypass tax on the sale of livestock, crops, machinery and equipment.

Using a CRT to sell appreciated property can:

- Bypass taxes on the sale
- Decrease other income taxes with charitable deductions and credits
- Increase annual income for retirement
- Reduce or eliminate estate tax
- Increase wealth passed to heirs
- Create legacy gifts to favorite charities

How It Works

You (the donor) establish a Charitable Remainder Trust (CRT) and transfer assets (e.g., land, livestock, crops, machinery, equipment) to the trust, removing the assets' values from your estate. The trustee of the CRT then sells the assets and, since the trust is a tax-exempt entity, there are no income taxes due upon the sale. The proceeds from the sale are then invested within the trust in a manner designed to provide a lifetime income for the beneficiaries. Two sets of beneficiaries are established, the income beneficiaries (generally the donor and his or her spouse), and the remainder beneficiaries (the charity or charities that will receive whatever assets remain in the trust after the income beneficiaries die.)

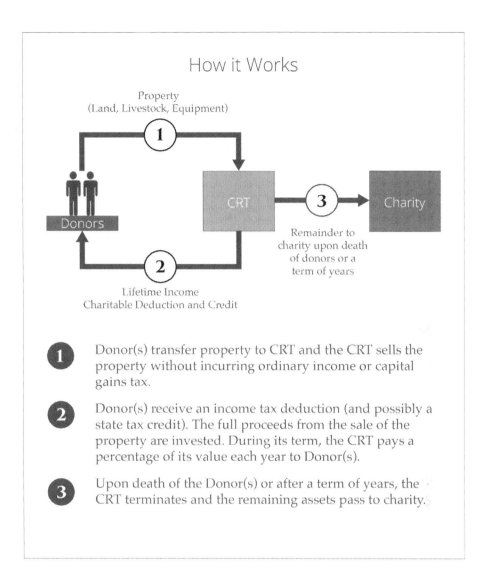

The Golden Goose

A CRT effectively allows you to convert your appreciated land into a lifetime income stream without incurring income taxes on the sale. By selling a farm or ranch through a CRT, you are essentially giving away the Golden Goose but reserving the right to the Golden Eggs it lays for the rest of your lives. If you sell without a CRT, you get to keep the goose but because the IRS cuts off its wings and feet, it is not able to produce as large of eggs.

Common Reasons Given For Not Using a CRT

Section 664 of the Internal Revenue Code authorizing charitable remainder trusts was added to the tax code in 1969, as part of the Tax Reform Act of 1969. This financial tool has been available for a long time and is used extensively by those selling highly appreciated assets. If you've ever watched Public Broadcasting Service (PBS) on TV, you've likely seen how funding for their program is often provided by people's CRTs.

Some people think you need to be very wealthy or sophisticated to use CRTs. This is simply not true. If you have appreciated property and desire to save taxes on the sale of your property and generate lifetime retirement income, you owe it to yourself to investigate what a CRT can offer.

It is important that you speak to someone who has extensive experience with CRTs and farm and ranch sales. Do not just rely on the advice of your trusted advisor if he or she only has limited experience. If you are selling a highly appreciated farm or ranch, get a comparison analysis done from someone that specializes in farm and ranch CRTs showing you what the tax savings and other benefits would be as compared to an outright sale. Numbers don't lie (assuming the analysis is done correctly) and this analysis will help you determine if a CRT makes sense for you and your situation.

It is perplexing to me, and other experienced CPAs and estate planning attorneys I've spoken with, that more agricultural families do not use a CRT to sell their appreciated property. After clearly seeing how they would be better off financially by selling their property through a CRT, many agriculture families still opt not to use this powerful tool. In my experience, families have given these reasons for not using a CRT:

1. It is more complicated than an outright sale.
2. Fear and distrust of working with advisors.
3. Negative feedback from CPAs or other trusted advisors who do not have extensive experience with CRTs.
4. Loss of control - no access to principal.
5. No charitable intent.
6. Concern about how the sales proceeds will be invested.

I'll address each of these six reasons below.

First, the sale of a ranch is a complicated process with or without a CRT. Most of the steps you have to take in selling a farm or ranch with a CRT you have to do anyway. Adding a CRT to the process of selling a farm or ranch does involve more work, but it also brings in new people to help you work through the sale planning process. The question you should ask yourself is, are these extra steps worth it?

Second, in my experience, most agricultural families like simplicity. While they are very savvy in managing their farm and ranch, they are usually not very savvy when it comes to financial planning. Many are reluctant to seek out and pay for professional help. While most farmers and ranchers hate paying taxes with a passion, they are often uncomfortable using what they view as complex financial strategies. And, because some are distrustful of advisors and are used to doing things by themselves, they seek out the simplest and safest solution when selling their property and retiring. This typically means paying taxes and investing the after-tax proceeds conservatively, typically in CDs.

Third, farmers and ranchers often turn to their trusted advisors when seeking input on whether or not to use a CRT. Unfortunately, many advisors do not have much experience with planned giving strategies such as a CRT. Because of this, some of these advisors discourage their clients from using a CRT to prevent themselves from looking incompetent or because it may require them to perform research or other work that they may not be able to bill for. Most farmers and ranchers are used to paying a certain amount for their tax preparation each year. If a CPA has to do work which they cannot bill for, they may be inclined to discourage use of a CRT, especially when they do not understand the benefits.

In my experience, farmers and ranchers tend to be very loyal people. I greatly respect this loyalty but sometimes it can be to their detriment. I'll never forget meeting with a CPA and one of his clients who was selling a highly appreciated ranch. The CRT would have saved this family close to $1 million but because the CPA was not experienced with CRTs, he said to his client, "Are you sure you want to jump through all those hoops?" I couldn't believe what I was hearing! This was a family that had worked hard for fifty years on their ranch and their CPA was asking them if it was worth saving $1 million to do a little extra work! Sadly, the family decided not to use the CRT because their CPA wasn't comfortable with it. Remember, you're the one that will have to write the check to the IRS, not your CPA or other advisor. If your advisor is not experienced with CRTs, find one that is.

Fourth, loss of control / no access to principal. If you sell property through a CRT, you do not have access to those sale proceeds; rather, you receive a percentage of those proceeds that are invested inside the trust each year for the rest of your lives.

In my experience, most families that have done an outright sale of their property and invested the after-tax proceeds from the sale rarely access the principal anyway. Their main goal is to generate income for the remainder of their lives. They take monthly or quarterly distributions from the portfolio and have them deposited directly into their checking account.

Money invested in a CRT is normally invested the same way as it is outside a CRT. Distributions from the portfolio in a CRT are handled in a similar manner as investments held outside a CRT.

The point I am trying to make is that it often doesn't make sense to pay 25% or more of the sales price in taxes just so you can have access to principal. If you need or want access to money besides the monthly income you receive from a CRT, it may be better to take some cash out of the sale and invest that money in a separate account. A great thing about combining a direct sale for cash with a CRT is that you may be able to completely wipe out the tax on your cash proceeds through the charitable tax deduction you receive from donating your property to the CRT.

Fifth, no charitable intent. A CRT makes the most sense for people who are selling highly appreciated assets and who also have a desire to give to charitable causes. With today's high tax rates, however, a CRT often makes sense financially even if you have little charitable intent. In other words, you and your family may be financially better off in the short run and the long run selling through a CRT than not selling through a CRT. If you are charitably motivated and you give money to charity anyway, a CRT can be a far more cost-effective and impactful way to give than giving cash or leaving money to charity through your will.

Sixth, fear of what happens to your money. Some people are afraid to utilize a CRT to sell their property because they fear what happens to their money. They're afraid the trustee of the CRT could run off with their money or they fear that if the trustee goes broke, their funds will be lost.

If you are concerned about the trustee of your CRT not handling your money responsibly and you want to maintain control over how your money is invested, you can be the trustee yourself. Most people who establish a CRT choose to use an outside trustee because they do not want to be bothered with the duties of the trustee and because some charitable organizations will serve as trustee for free if they are named as one of the remainder beneficiaries.

It is important to understand that a charitable organization serving as the trustee of your CRT doesn't have ownership of the money. The trustee's job is to serve as a fiduciary. The money invested inside a CRT is usually held in a custodial account with reputable custodians such as TD Ameritrade or Charles Schwab. If the trustee managing your CRT stops serving as trustee for whatever reason, you simply take over as trustee yourself or find another organization to serve as trustee.

My advice to those families selling a highly appreciated ranch is to speak with someone that has extensive experience with ranch sales and CRTs who can help you determine if a CRT makes sense for you. Provide them with the facts of your situation and have them run an illustration showing you the potential benefits. You should also try to speak to clients that have used CRTs with the sale of their farm or ranch property.

"But What About My Children?"

A common concern among those using a CRT is replacing the wealth that ultimately passes to charity instead of their heirs. This begs the question, is there a way to use a CRT without disinheriting the children? The answer is yes.

For those who wish to use a CRT with the sale of their property and who also wish to replace the value of the assets they donate to a CRT for their children, there are strategies you can use. Some of these strategies may allow you to actually increase the amount of wealth passed to your heirs.

A common "wealth replacement" strategy employed with a CRT is using a portion of the payments from the CRT to purchase life insurance. Premiums for life insurance can often be paid out of the "excess" income generated from the CRT. When I say "excess" income, I am referring to the additional income the donors receive from investing the full sales proceeds rather than the after-tax proceeds.

In using this wealth replacement strategy, donors use payments they receive from the CRT each year to pay premiums on a life insurance policy on their lives with their children and/or grandchildren named as beneficiaries. When the donors die, the charitable organizations named as remainder beneficiaries get what's left in the CRT and the children of the donors receive the proceeds of the life insurance.

And, if the life insurance is set up in an irrevocable life insurance trust (ILIT), the life insurance proceeds are received by your children income and estate tax-free.

Survivorship Life Insurance

Survivorship life insurance, also known as Second-to-Die Life insurance, is a type of policy that insures two lives under one policy with the death benefit paid out on the second death. Survivorship life insurance is commonly used with CRTs and other estate planning situations because estate taxes are typically not due until the second spouse's death. Survivorship life insurance is less costly than a single life policy and if one spouse doesn't qualify for life insurance due to health conditions, a Survivorship life insurance policy can typically be purchased if the other spouse is healthy.

Irrevocable Life Insurance Trust

There are ownership issues associated with life insurance that impacts whether or not the death benefit proceeds are included in an estate. If there are "incidents of ownership" in the policy, it will be included in a person's estate. Incidents of ownership can include the right to borrow on a policy's cash value, to change the policy's beneficiary, to change a settlement option, and change the dividend selection. If the insured person(s) retains outright ownership or incidents of ownership in the policy, the proceeds of the policy would be brought into the estate for estate tax purposes. However, when an irrevocable life insurance trust (ILIT) owns a life insurance policy

How it Works

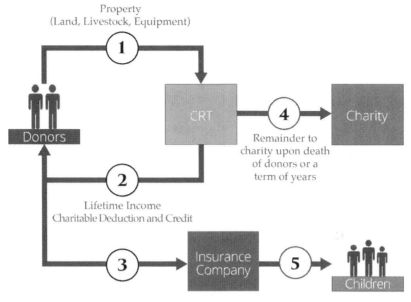

1 Donors transfer property (land, crops, livestock, machinery, equipment) to CRT.

2 Donors receive an income tax deduction (and possibly a state tax credit) and pay no ordinary or capital gains tax on the sale by the trust. The full proceeds from the sale of the property are invested.

During its term, which is typically the Donor(s) lifetime, the trust pays a percentage of its value each year to Donor(s).

3 Donor(s) pay annual life insurance premiums to an insurance company. If an ILIT is used, donors gift the amount needed to pay the annual premium to the trustee of the ILIT and the trustee pays the premiums.

4 Upon the death of the surviving donor, the CRT terminates and the remaining assets in CRT pass to charity.

5 Upon the death of the surviving Donor, the life insurance death benefits are paid to the heirs.

and the payments are structured properly, the death proceeds can be received by the family income tax free and not be included in the insured's taxable estate.

Instead of using life insurance to replace wealth for children, another option is to open a separate investment account for your children and gift money that you receive from the CRT each year into this account. Life insurance is typically preferred to using a separate investment account because life insurance can guarantee your children a sum of money if you die prematurely whereas an investment account may take years to grow to the amount of money you wish to replace for your kids.

CRT Sale vs. Direct Sale For Cash

In many cases today, the sale of appreciated property through a CRT not only provides a low cost gift to charity, but also leaves the donor's family better off.

On the following pages is a comparison of how selling appreciated land through a CRT can provide benefits over a direct sale. As you can see, in this example, by using a CRT to sell a highly appreciated ranch, a family actually comes out ahead by roughly $550,000 over the parent's life expectancy by selling their property through a CRT. Instead of paying $442,243 to the government, they received $150,161 back from it – and, they leave a large gift to charity upon their death.

Option 1: Outright Sale

Outright sale for cash of real property valued at $2,000,000 with a $200,000 cost basis

Option 2: Charitable Remainder Trust

Sale of the property through a CRT

Comparison Summary	Outright Sale	CRT Sale
Gross Sales Proceeds	$2,000,000	2,000,000
Taxes Paid On Sale	($442,243)	$0
Taxes Saved from Charitable Deduction/Credit	$0	$150,161
After-Tax Estate to Heirs:	$5,795,518	$6,588,350
Amount to Charity on Death:	$0	$1,414,908

Illustration Summary

Sale of Real Property: 1000 acres @ $2,000/acre	Assumed Rates	Outright Sale	Contribute Land to CRT
Sale Price - Inside CRT			**$2,000,000**
Cost of Sale			$144,000
Net Sale Proceeds to CRT			$1,856,000
Donor costs of contribution to CRT[1] (appraisal/closing costs)			($8,000)
Sales Price - Outside CRT		**$2,000,000**	
Basis		($200,000)	
Cost of Sale		($145,000)	
Capital Gain Outside CRT		$1,655,000	
Combined Capital Gain/Medicare Surtax Rates:[2]			
$0 - 250,000	19.9%	($49,750)	
$250,001 - $464,850	23.7%	($50,919)	
$464,851 -	28.7%	($341,574)	
Total Capital Gain/Medicare Tax		($442,243)	$0
Tax savings from Deduction/Credit			$150,161
TOTAL TAXES (DUE)/SAVED:[3]		**($442,243)**	**$150,161**
After tax proceeds:			
Outside trust		$1,412,758	$142,161
Inside CRT			$1,856,000
TOTAL AFTER-TAX PROCEEDS:		$1,412,758	$1,998,161
Proceeds invested to achieve 5% capital appreciation & 2% ordinary income annually for 27 yrs, after-tax			
Outside CRT		$5,795,518	$583,185
From CRT (8% annual payout rate)			$6,005,165
Charitable Deduction:[4]			$456,500
Fed Tax Savings	25.0%		$102,113
Montana Tax Savings:			
Endowment Tax Credit			$20,000
(40% of Charitable Deduction up to $10,000 per person)			
Excess Deduction	6.9%		$28,049
TOTAL TAX SAVINGS:			$150,161
COMPARISON OF BENEFITS			
After-Tax Proceeds with Investment Earnings Reinvested		**$5,795,518**	**$6,588,350**
Amount to Charity on Death		**$0**	**$1,414,908**
Taxes (Due)/Saved on Sale		**($442,243)**	**$150,161**

Assumptions

Donors ages 68 & 69
Life Expectancy 25 years

1. Costs do not include any of Donor's professional advisor fees.
2. Medicare Surtax does not apply to capital gain on the sale of land in certain cases.
3. Outright sale illustration does not include higher taxes from phase-out of personal exemptions and itemized deductions.
4. Calculated using AFR rate of 2.4%.

Source: Kurt Alme; Yellowstone Boys and Girls Ranch Foundation

The illustrations are based on the facts and assumptions stated above and are used for illustrative purposes only. The tax rates, investment returns and cost assumptions will vary. Please consult your own legal and tax advisors for specific results applicable to you.

Partial CRT Sale

Some people mistakenly think they must sell their entire farm or ranch through a CRT. This is not true. In fact, I rarely advise a family to sell all their property through a CRT. It is often best to take some cash out of a sale for debt pay-off and liquidity purposes.

A portion of land and / or livestock and equipment may be contributed to and sold by a CRT with the rest of the property sold for cash, and / or through a 1031 exchange. Combining a CRT with a cash sale and a 1031 exchange may offer the best combination of benefits. Besides bypassing tax on the sale of appreciated property, the donors receive an income tax deduction from their gift. This tax deduction enables a family to greatly reduce the income taxes due on cash they take out of a sale. To see an illustration of this combined strategy, see the Tax Reduction Wheel of Fortune in chapter six.

Besides saving taxes on a sale, an often overlooked benefit of a CRT is the enhanced asset diversification it can provide. When a family uses a 1031 exchange to save tax on the sale of their property, they often exchange into one or two commercial properties. This may not provide sufficient diversification. Conversely, a family may invest in a broadly diversified portfolio of securities within a CRT and rebalance the portfolio on a regular basis without paying capital gains taxes.

Types Of Charitable Remainder Trusts

There are two primary types of charitable trusts: the Charitable Remainder Annuity Trust (CRAT) and the Charitable Remainder Unitrust (CRUT).

The Charitable Remainder Annuity Trust

A charitable remainder annuity trust pays a fixed dollar amount each year to the beneficiaries. The trust continues for the life of all income recipients, or for a specified term of years not to exceed 20. Upon the death of all income beneficiaries or the end of the specified term, the remainder goes to the charity or charities named. Since charitable remainder annuity trusts provide a fixed amount paid out each year, this type of trust cannot take advantage of future earnings in excess of the annual payments. However, this trust does offer the security of consistent payments, even in a flat or down market. Due to the fixed payout obligation, additional contributions to an existing CRAT are not allowed.

Here is an example of a Charitable Remainder Annuity Trust income stream with a hypothetical investment portfolio and a 7% payout:

CRAT Payout 7%			
Year	Earnings Rate	Trust Value	Annuity Amount
1	8%	$1,000,000	$ 70,000
2	6%	$1,010,000	$ 70,000
3	10%	$1,000,600	$ 70,000
4	8%	$1,030,660	$ 70,000
5	4%	$1,043,113	$ 70,000
6	12%	$1,014,837	$ 70,000
7	6%	$1,066,618	$ 70,000
8	7%	$1,060,615	$ 70,000
9	3%	$1,064,858	$ 70,000
10		$1,026,804	$ 70,000

The Charitable Remainder Unitrust

The charitable remainder unitrust pays a fixed percentage of the trust's value each year. The donor selects the percentage at the time the trust is created. The percentage must be at least five percent but not more than the percentage which allows at least 10 percent to pass to charity. Following the death of the lifetime beneficiaries, or the end of the term, the remaining trust property goes to the charity or charities named. Unlike the charitable remainder annuity trust, additional contributions to CRUTs are permitted.

Here is an example of a standard Charitable Remainder Unitrust income stream with the same investment earnings and payout rate as the CRAT.

Year	CRUT Payout 7%		
	Earnings Rate	Trust Value	Annuity Amount
1	8%	$1,000,000	$ 70,000
2	6%	$1,010,000	$ 70,700
3	10%	$ 999,900	$ 69,993
4	8%	$1,029,897	$ 72,093
5	4%	$1,040,196	$ 72,814
6	12%	$1,008,990	$ 70,629
7	6%	$1,059,440	$ 74,161
8	7%	$1,048,845	$ 73,419
9	3%	$1,048,845	$ 73,419
10		$1,006,891	$ 70,482

Tax Benefits From Contribution Of Land To A CRT

Tax savings are one of the main benefits of charitable remainder trusts. Here are the potential tax benefits from contributing land to a CRT:

An Immediate Income Tax Deduction

Donors of land to a CRT receive an immediate income tax deduction based on the present value of the charity's remainder interest. The amount of the tax deduction depends on factors such as the fair market value of the trust property donated to the CRT, the amount of the annuity or the percentage of trust assets paid annually by the CRT, the age of those receiving income from the CRT and discount rates set by the IRS.

If you choose a high payout from your CRT, you receive a low charitable income tax deduction. Conversely, if you select a low payout from your CRT, you receive a high charitable income tax deduction.

The charitable deduction can be used to offset income tax in the year of the gift, and any unused deduction can be carried forward up to five years. If appreciated property is donated, the deduction each year is limited to 30% of the donor's adjusted gross income.

Many people choose to leave assets to charity upon their death. While gifts to charity upon death reduce the value of an estate and may help reduce estate taxes, the income tax benefits can only offset income in your estate. The advantage of donating assets to a CRT during your lifetime is you not only reduce the value of your estate for estate tax purposes, you also immediately benefit from an income tax deduction.

State Income Tax Credit

Some states offer a tax credit for charitable planned giving. In Montana, contributions to a CRT restricted to charitable endowments are eligible for a state income tax credit. Montana's tax credit, called the Montana Income Tax Credit for Endowed Philanthropy, provides a credit against state income tax liability in the amount of 40% of the present value of any planned gift (which includes CRTs) made to a permanent endowment of a Montana charity up to a maximum amount of $10,000 per year per taxpayer.

A strategy used by some taxpayers is to donate the maximum amount of assets to a CRT each year to fully benefit from this tax credit.

Taxes Bypassed On Sale

Assets contributed to a CRT can be sold free of any income tax and Medicare Surtax to the donor. This is particularly significant if the real estate is highly appreciated. By saving capital gains tax, the money that would have gone to paying tax can be invested to generate income for retirement.

Federal Estate Tax Savings

Assets contributed to a CRT will not be subject to tax in the donor's estate. Thus, future estate tax may be reduced or avoided entirely. Also, the CRT is not subject to executor's fees or other probate costs.

CRT Is Income Tax Exempt

A CRT itself is tax-exempt and pays no income tax or Medicare Surtax on interest, dividends, rents or capital gain.

Taxation of Income From a CRT

Income donors receive from a CRT retains the character it had inside the CRT. Each payment is taxable in one of four categories, in the following order of priority:

First, as ordinary income to the extent of the CRT's accumulated ordinary income. Second, as capital gains to the extent of the CRT's accumulated capital gains. Third, as tax-exempt income to the extent of the CRT's accumulated exempt income. Fourth, as tax-free return of principal.

Trustees of CRT's will provide you with a Form K-1 showing you how to report the CRT payments on your tax return.

Selling Livestock, Crops And Equipment In A CRT

Land is not the only asset you can contribute to a CRT. Livestock, crops, machinery and equipment can also contributed.

Sale Of Calves And Crops

Proceeds from the sale of calves and crops are treated as ordinary income and incur self-employment tax (Social Security tax and Medicare tax). The same calves and crops sold in a CRT will defer the income tax and avoid the self-employment taxes otherwise due on the sale. This allows the full proceeds from the sale of the calves and crops to be invested inside the CRT to generate lifetime income for the donors. Contribution of calves and crops to a CRT generally does not generate a charitable income tax to the donor.

Sale Of Cows

Breeding livestock such as cows are capital assets and incur capital gains tax on sales. The same cows sold in a CRT will avoid or defer this tax. This allows the full proceeds from the sale of the cows to be invested inside the CRT to generate lifetime income for the donors. Contribution of cows generates a charitable deduction based on the donor's basis in them.

Sale Of Equipment

The recapture of depreciation on the sale of machinery, equipment or other depreciated personal property is treated as ordinary income. These same assets sold through a CRT will avoid or defer this tax, permitting the full proceeds to be invested to generate lifetime income for the donors. Contribution of machinery or equipment generates a charitable deduction based on the donor's basis in it.

Using A CRT For Damage Mitigation

Sometimes a family learns about the benefits of a CRT after it is too late. That is, after they either sold their property or after they have a signed buy-sell agreement. If you have a signed buy-sell agreement, you will most likely not be able to utilize a CRT. Some people have asked, "Why can't we just tear up this buy-sell and create a new one with the CRT?" The problem with this is that the IRS could view this as a "pre-arranged sale" and disallow the tax savings generated by the CRT.

If you have sold your property and you now are in shock from the tax bill, you may be able to create a CRT and contribute cash to the CRT as a means of damage mitigation. Contributing cash to a CRT will generate a charitable income tax deduction and you can use this deduction to reduce the taxes you have due on the sale.

How High Can The CRT Payout Be?

Statutory rules prohibit CRT payouts in excess of 50% of the contributed property and mandate that the percentage must be low enough to ensure that the present value of the interest which passes to charity upon the conclusion of your life (or the selected term) is at least 10% of each contribution to the CRT. This 10% rule only applies when you contribute assets to the CRT. As long as the 10% rule is met at the creation of the CRT, it doesn't matter if the amount in the trust at a later time falls under 10%.

In addition, rules require the CRT payout be no lower than 5%. CRT payouts are determined using an "Applicable Federal Government Interest Rate" at the time of contribution to the CRT and either the age of the income beneficiaries – if the trust is guaranteed for life, or the length of the term – if the trust payout is for a selected period of years.

Generally, you should not select a payout percentage that is too high because if the CRT pays out too much income each year, it will deplete the principal inside the trust and you may receive less income over your life expectancy than you would if you had chosen a lower payout. A good financial advisor working together with a planned giving specialist will help you calculate a payout percentage that is appropriate for you.

Can The Payout Extend Past My Lifetime?

CRT payments can extend beyond the donors' lifetimes. This can be achieved by creating a term of years charitable remainder trust that happens to "outlive" the donor(s), or setting the trust term as lives plus a term of years. The second option (and perhaps the first, depending on ages) would reduce the charitable deduction, and if the settlor does not retain the right to terminate the successor beneficiaries' interests, there will be a taxable gift to those beneficiaries at the time the trust is created. Finally, adding beneficiaries other than a spouse, results in a loss of the marital deduction potentially causing additional taxable gifts.

Who Should Be The Trustee Of Your CRT?

While you are not prevented from serving as trustee of your CRT, it often is better to name another person because you will be subject to some additional restrictions. You can either name another individual, such as a family member, to serve as trustee or appoint a corporate trustee to serve. Many people choose a corporate trustee because they have more investment and administrative expertise. A charitable organization may be able to serve as trustee (sometimes without charge) if irrevocably named as a remainder beneficiary. Regardless of who you select as trustee, however, you can retain the ability to remove and replace the trustee at any time during the term of the CRT.

Can I Change The Remainder Beneficiaries?

Most CRTs are drafted to allow the donors to change the charitable remainder beneficiaries named in the trust document at any time during their life. A CRT can also be drafted to require you to irrevocably designate a specific charity as a remainder beneficiary for all or part of the CRT.

Appraisals

If you wish to use a CRT for the sale of your property, an appraisal must be completed by a qualified appraiser. The appraisal establishes the value of the trust for the tax deduction. Appraisals must be completed no earlier than 60 days before the trust is funded and not later than the date the income tax return is due.

Debt On Property And CRTs

Contributing property which secures debt causes several issues and should be avoided if at all possible.

If you have debt secured by property you wish to donate to a CRT, you have a few options. If you have other liquid resources, one option is to pay off the debt before donating the property to a CRT. The second option is to secure the debt with other collateral. Banks will normally release a security interest on a portion of land going into a CRT if the loan holders have been paying on the loan a long time and if sufficient collateral remains to provide adequate security. The third option is to get a bridge loan to pay off the secured debt.

Pre-Arranged Sale

The IRS does not allow you to avoid income tax on the sale of property contributed to a CRT if the sale was pre-arranged prior to contribution. Generally, the IRS looks to see if the trustee of the CRT is obligated to sell the assets as part of a pre-arranged sale in determining whether to attribute the gain to the donor or the CRT. While some negotiation of an upcoming sale will not likely cause you to be responsible for paying tax on the gain, it is imperative that no binding contract be finalized. It is best to transfer property to a CRT as early as possible in the negotiations.

CRTs And Ranch Brokers

In most ranch brokers' eyes, all you are doing by adding a CRT to a farm or ranch sale is introducing complication to their world. They care about selling your property, not saving you taxes on the sale. While it is true that you do not want to do something that will make your property less marketable by doing something to hinder a sale, a CRT should not impact a sale or sale price. As long as you are working with an experienced team, selling all or part of your property through a CRT should not be difficult and should proceed smoothly.

Unlike a Conservation Easement, for example, a CRT doesn't have any impact on the buyer's use of the land. The ranch broker you are working with will still market the property as he or she would if a CRT wasn't involved. The ranch broker will simply let the buyer know that the ranch is being sold through a CRT for tax purposes. If you are selling part of your ranch in an outright sale and part through a CRT, your buyer will have two buy-sell agreements, one with you and one with the trustee of your CRT.

You are potentially paying a farm/ranch broker a lot of money to sell your property. They work for you, not the other way around. If you want to utilize a CRT to save taxes on the sale, you need to find a reputable broker who will work with you to accomplish this goal.

If you are a ranch broker reading this, becoming knowledgeable about how to work with CRTs and farm/ranch sales can help you set yourself apart from other brokers. A satisfied customer is more likely to say good things about you and refer you to other clients if you have shown a willingness to work with them to accomplish their financial goals.

Summary

A charitable remainder trust is a powerful strategy for saving tax on the sale of a farm or ranch. It enables a family to save taxes on the sale of land, livestock, crops and equipment and generate income for retirement.

A CRT involves extra steps that must be done before a sales contract is signed. It is critical to work with a team that has extensive experience in using CRTs for farm and ranch sales.

For those concerned about replacing assets donated to a CRT for their children, life insurance can be a good solution.

There are two types of charitable remainder trusts: The Charitable Remainder Annuity Trust and the Charitable Remainder Unitrust. A CRAT pays a fixed dollar amount each year to the beneficiaries. The CRUT pays a fixed percentage of the trust's value each year.

The most significant consideration when establishing a charitable remainder trust is the choice of the annuity or payout rate. This choice will affect not only the amount of income you receive, but it will also affect the amount of the donor's charitable deduction. The payout rate may also influence what investments are to be used in the trust.

A CRT can be combined with a 1031 exchange and/or outright sale. This strategy can be a powerful way to optimize tax savings and provide liquidity and investment diversification.

Like any income or estate tax saving tool, there is some work involved in administering a CRT. The creation of a CRT involves the drafting of the trust document, appraising the assets to be transferred, and transferring them into the CRT. Annual tax returns need to be filed for the trust, form K-1s need to be given to the beneficiaries, and appropriate distributions must be made each year. Some charities will serve as trustee at no charge if they are named a remainder beneficiary. They may also help you set up the trust, transfer the assets and file annual tax returns all at no charge.

CHAPTER 5

Other Sale Planning Issues And Opportunities

This chapter will cover some common issues and opportunities that arise when selling a farm or ranch.

Owning Farm And Ranch Real Estate Inside An Entity

How you own your farm or ranch impacts the tax treatment and planning options available to you.

While it is possible to utilize a 1031 exchange and a charitable remainder trust with properties owned in an entity, using these tools with an entity has other planning ramifications.

Property Owned In a C Corporation

While most farmers and ranchers own their property in an LLC, partnership or S corporation, some families still own property in a C corporation. A C corporation is a separate taxable entity and pays tax on income at the corporate level. When a C corporation sells appreciated real estate, it must pay tax on the gain at the corporate tax rate. When proceeds from the sale are then distributed to the shareholders as dividends, the shareholders will also have to pay tax on this income at their personal tax rate. Due to this double taxation, the total tax due from the sale of appreciated real estate in a C corporation could easily exceed 50%.

One way to avoid the double taxation is to sell the stock of the corporation rather than the assets of the corporation. The buyer, however, usually prefers to buy the land not the stock because they do not want to inherit any potential liabilities of the corporation. Examples of potential liabilities they could inherit from buying the stock versus buying the land are past environmental issues, lawsuits with neighbors or liens on the property. Because of this, a seller may have to significantly discount their sales price in order to entice a buyer. This is not something most farmers and ranchers are eager to do.

C Corporation 1031 Exchange

One way to potentially avoid this double tax consequence is for the C corporation to perform a 1031 exchange. While it is not normally advised to perform a 1031 exchange on the total sale value, this is one situation where it may make sense to consider an exchange for the entire property. If shareholders in a C-corporation desire to go their separate ways as part of an exchange by the C-corporation there are hurdles. However, solutions such as "spin-offs" or "split-ups" may be worthy of some discussion with tax professionals.

Converting From C Corporation To S Corporation Status

Under the 1986 Tax Act, personal rates were reduced and C corporations were permitted to convert to an S corporation, thereby avoiding the double tax. However, some C corporation shareholders never took the opportunity to convert.

A potential solution to avoid the double taxation on future liquidation of real estate in a C corporation is to convert the C corporation to an S corporation. In order to become an S corporation, a C corporation must file IRS Form 2553 with the IRS. This form must be signed by all shareholders. Approval of Form 2553 by the IRS is routine (not discretionary) as long as the corporation meets the formal eligibility requirements.

Built-In-Gain Tax And Five-Year Holding Period

S corporations that were once C corporations are potentially subject to the Built-In-Gain (BIG) tax. Under the BIG tax, an S corporation could be subject to tax on gains from the sale of assets held at the time it converted to S corporation status if it sells the assets within a five year period after making its S election (the recognition period).

A holding period exists for conversions from C corporations to S corporations. This holding period was previously ten years. Fortunately, in December of 2015, Congress made the 5-year recognition period for built-in gains permanent. If the S corporation sells appreciated property prior to this 5-year holding period, a BIG tax may be imposed. This tax is imposed at the highest corporate tax rate, currently 35%.

The BIG Tax ends after the S corporation's fifth tax year. Therefore, you can avoid the BIG tax if the unrecognized built-in gains are not recognized until after the fifth year as an S corporation. In other words, by performing a 1031 exchange at the C corporation level and holding the real estate until the expiration of the BIG tax's five-year holding requirement period, it may be possible to liquidate real estate now held in the S corporation and avoid tax at the corporate level.

Charitable Remainder Trust And C Corporations

There are two options for selling a farm and ranch owned in a C corporation with a CRT.

1. Contribute stock to CRT. This solution works best for the taxpayer. In this case, the CRT tries to sell the stock to the buyer instead of the land. Again, buyers usually prefer to buy the land instead of the stock so this option is not often used.

2. Contribute land to the CRT. The C corporation contributes land to a CRT (the C corporation is the donor) and have the trustee of the CRT sell the land. Because a corporation does not have a life expectancy, the payout from the CRT cannot

be for the donor's lifetime. Instead, it has to be for a period of years, not to exceed twenty.

A significant question you face in this situation is if you transfer the stock, are you going to be substantially liquidating the corporation? This is known as the substantial liquidation rule. If you trigger the substantial liquidation rule, you have to pay tax on the sale of the land whether you put the stock into a CRT or not. The IRS has not issued clear guidelines on what represents a substantial liquidation. Commentators say if you liquidate more than 60% to 80%, it will likely be considered a substantial liquidation.

The issues involved in planning for a 1031 exchange or charitable remainder trust with a C corporation are somewhat complex. Make sure you seek out expert assistance if your property is owned in a C corporation and you desire to use a 1031 exchange or charitable remainder trust to save tax on the sale of your property.

Charitable Remainder Trust And S Corporations

S corporation stock cannot be contributed to a CRT. A CRT is not a permitted shareholder of S corporation stock. If you put S corporation stock into a CRT, you will convert the S corporation into a C corporation. An S corporation, however, can contribute land into a CRT for term of years. The same substantial liquidation rule applies with an S corporation as with a C corporation.

Two other things to keep in mind when selling property owned in an S corporation are: 1. In order to use the charitable deduction with a gift of property to a CRT, the S corporation must be the charitable owner and 2. If an S corporation was previously a C corporation, it may create problems associated with built-in gains and passive income.

Conflicting Interests Among Entity Owners

Owning appreciated real estate in an entity can present challenges if there are multiple partners, members or shareholders with different goals upon sale. For example, if two people own appreciated land in partnership and one partner would like to use a 1031 exchange and one partner would like to pay tax and take the after-tax proceeds, there is a problem.

The IRC 1031 exchange provisions require that the entity selling the relinquished property must be the same entity taking title to the replacement property. So in this case, the partnership would have to perform the exchange and each partner could not do his or her own exchange. Fortunately, there are solutions to this problem.

Solution 1: Drop And Swap

Prior to a sale, the partnership could distribute (drop) the property out of the partnership. Each partner would take title to their ownership in the property as tenants-in-common. This would allow each partner to then perform a 1031 exchange (swap) for their ownership in the property if they so desired.

To comply with IRS rules, it is important that the distribution of the property out of the partnership take place well in advance of a sale. Please consult your CPA and/or attorney regarding this matter.

Solution 2: Swap And Drop

Using this strategy, the partners could each identify their own separate property (ies) they wish to own. The partnership would perform the exchange (swap) and at a later date, preferably longer than one year, the partnership could distribute the property (drop) to each partner "in-kind". Once again, consult your CPA and/or attorney regarding the use of this strategy.

Using A CRT With Multiple Partners With Conflicting Goals

There are a couple of options for selling property owned in a partnership through a CRT when there are conflicting goals of the partners. The first and best option is to terminate the partnership and distribute the land out to each partner in their respective ownership percentages. Land would be portioned off according to each partner's ownership amount and then each partner would take title to his own land. Each partner could then do whatever they wanted to do with the land they owned. If one wanted to do a CRT with their portion and the other wanted to do a 1031 exchange or outright sale, they could do that.

The advantage of this option is that the partners would not have to take a discount for an undivided interest in the property. If they did a CRT, they would be able to receive a charitable deduction for the fair market value of the property. The challenge with this option is that it may be difficult to partition the land into parcels representing each owner's share in the overall partnership.

The second option for a partner who wants to use a CRT with the sale of land owned in an LLC (or partnership) is contribute his or her percentage of the LLC membership interest to a CRT. Then, when a buyer comes along, the buyer buys part of the property from the CRT and part from the other owner.

The problem with this option is that if you put membership interests of an LLC into a CRT, an appraiser will likely discount the value for lack of marketability and perhaps only a minority interest. This discounted value means you get a lower charitable income deduction from your contribution to the CRT.

If you distribute property out of the LLC and put it all into the CRT, the value is not discounted and therefore, you receive a charitable deduction based upon the full fair market value of the property.

Selling Multiple Separately Deeded Parcels

A farm or ranch is often comprised of multiple separately deeded parcels. This typically occurs as a result of a family purchasing additional parcels of land over time. These different parcels usually have very different cost basis figures, depending on when they were acquired.

If a farm or ranch has multiple separately deeded parcels with different cost basis figures and a family is planning on performing a partial 1031 exchange or utilizing a charitable remainder trust, an effective tax-saving strategy is to exchange the low basis parcels or use a CRT for the low basis parcels and take cash out of the high basis parcels. To do this, it may be necessary to obtain separate buy-sell agreements on the different parcels.

Installment Sale

An installment sale, also known as a contract for deed, is another option available to families selling their farm or ranch. An installment sale involves a sale of property where you receive at least one payment after the tax year of the sale.

An installment sale can be advantageous to a seller because as the seller of the property, you can receive payments over a number of years. By having payments spread over a number of years, you may be able to receive some of the payments when you are in a lower tax bracket. An installment sale is attractive to a buyer because it allows them to obtain financing and make payments over a period of time at possibly lower interest rates than they could get at a bank.

Each payment on an installment sale usually consists of the following three parts. 1. Interest income. 2. Return of your adjusted basis in the property. 3. Gain on the sale. You, as the seller, need to make sure you separate the principal from interest on each installment. The interest portion must be reported as ordinary income.

When a payment is received, the amount reported as gain is the same percentage of the payment as the total gain is of the total sale price. For example, if a ranch sold for $5 million and the cost basis at the time of sale was $1 million (in this example, it is assumed there aren't any assets included in the sale that have been depreciated, because any gain due to depreciation has to be recaptured as ordinary income in the year of sale regardless of it being an installment sale), the gain would be $4 million or eighty percent of the sale price ($4 million divided by $5 million). If the buyer and seller agree to an installment sale, the buyer would need to report eighty percent of each installment payment as gain.

If you are considering an installment sale for your property, make sure that you receive a large down payment so that if the buyers default on their contract, you will not lose money if you have to take the property back and re-sell it. You also want to make sure you earn a competitive interest rates on your contract compared to the rate of return you could receive if you invested the cash yourself or if you did a 1031 exchange into other income producing real estate investments.

Installment Sales With 1031 Exchange Or Charitable Remainder Trust

It is possible to use a 1031 exchange and a CRT with an installment sale. There are, however, added complexities to doing so. If you are interested in combining a 1031 or CRT with an installment sale, make sure to consult with an experienced 1031 intermediary or planned giving specialist prior to the sale, as well as consulting with you attorney and CPA.

Life Estate Reserved

For those people interested in giving all or a portion of their farm or ranch to a charitable or conservation organization, a life estate reserved is a possible solution. A life estate reserved allows you to make a gift of all or a portion of your farm or ranch, receive a current federal income tax deduction for your gift and retain the right to use the property for your lifetime.

How It Works

You execute a deed transferring your property to a charity. In the deed, you retain a "life estate" that grants you the right to use the property for your life. You receive an income tax charitable deduction for your gift. The federal income tax deduction you receive is for the present value of the remainder interest in the property.

The life estate lasts for your lifetime or the life of you and another person. You are responsible for the maintenance, insurance and taxes while living on the property.

Combining a life estate reserved with other financial planning strategies may help landowners accomplish retirement and estate planning objectives. For example, you may have a need or desire to liquidate other appreciated property or to convert a traditional IRA to a Roth IRA. The income tax deduction you receive from the life estate may be used to offset tax on the liquidation of appreciated property or the tax on the Roth IRA conversion.

A life estate reserved is almost always a better option than leaving the property to charity through your will because the life estate reserved generates an immediate charitable deduction.

Conservation Easement

A conservation easement may allow an agricultural family to receive cash from their property while continuing to live on and operate their farm or ranch. You can sell a conservation easement for cash or if you are mainly looking for a tax deduction, you can gift the conservation easement.

A conservation easement is a deed restriction landowners voluntarily place on their property to protect resources such as productive farmland, wildlife habitat, ground and surface water, historic sites or scenic views. You may have no intention to develop your property but if you want to make sure your property is preserved forever, a conservation easement can be appealing. An easement binds your heirs and anyone else who purchases your property in the future from developing your land. Most easements "run with the land," so even if your property is later sold or passed on to heirs, it binds the original owner and all subsequent owners to the easement's restrictions.

You may be required to adhere to certain restrictions of an easement such as developing the property although you may reserve the right to build a house on the property for one of your children. You may also be required to perform certain tasks to protect the property such as fencing off areas to keep livestock out.

Tax consequences Of Conservation Easements

A conservation easement may offer a number of tax benefits for a farm or ranch owner. You may qualify for a federal charitable deduction. Any unused deduction can be carried forward five years beyond the year of the gift. The gift of an easement may qualify for an estate tax exclusion for a portion of the value of the underlying land that is subject to a conservation easement, thereby reducing the your taxable estate and potential estate taxes.

Some states offer dollar-for-dollar tax credits to landowners who make gifts of conservation easements or who sell conservation easements and some states offer local real property tax benefits for landowners who convey conservation easements on their lands.

IRC Section 121 Principal Residence Exclusion

IRC Section 121 allows an individual to exclude up to $250,000 of taxable gain from the sale of a principal residence and a married couple filing a joint return to exclude up to $500,000 of gain. This exclusion can only be used in conjunction with real property that has been held and used as the homeowner's primary residence. It does not apply to second homes, vacation homes, or property that has been held for rental, investment or use in a trade or business.

Homeowners are required to have owned and lived in the home as their primary residence for at least a combined total of 24 months out of the last 60 months (two out of the last five years) in order to qualify for the principal residence exclusion. The 24 months does not have to be consecutive.

If your home is included in the sale of your farm or ranch, it may be wise to assign as much value as legally possible to the home so you can maximize the amount of tax-free proceeds from the sale. It is possible to include additional acreage around the home when determining a value for the home as long as the acreage does not include other buildings used for business purposes. Make sure to discuss this strategy with your real estate agent and CPA.

Oftentimes the home where a family resides on the farm or ranch is owned by the same entity that owns the other ranch property. A home owned by an entity is not eligible for the principal residence exclusion.

Summary

How you own your farm or ranch impacts the tax treatment and planning options available to you.

While it is possible to utilize a 1031 exchange and a CRT with properties owned in an entity, using these tools with an entity has other planning ramifications.

Due to the double taxation of a C corporation, taxes due on the sale of appreciated property owned in a C corporation can easily exceed fifty percent. A common solution used with people who own property in a C corporation and who wish to sell is to convert the C corporation to an S corporation. The property would then be sold using a 1031 exchange. If the property is held for at least five years after electing the S corporation status, the property can be sold and incur tax at only the shareholder level.

Owning appreciated real estate in an entity can present challenges if there are multiple owners with different goals upon sale. Two common solutions used are to either distribute property out of the entity and then exchange properties or to exchange into properties for each owner and then distribute the properties out of the entity to each owner.

A potential tax-saving strategy for someone selling multiple parcels with different cost basis figures and who desires to take some cash out of a sale is to use a CRT or 1031 exchange for the low basis parcels and to do an outright sale for cash on the high basis parcels.

An installment sale involves a sale of property where you receive at least one payment after the tax year of the sale. It can be an effective way to defer tax on a sale. It is possible to combine a 1031 exchange or CRT with an installment sale.

Conservation easements and life estate reserved are two other tax and estate planning tools that are commonly used with farm and ranch properties. A life estate reserved allows you to make a gift of all or a portion of your farm or ranch, receive a current income tax deduction for your gift and retain the right to use the property for your lifetime. A conservation easement may allow an agricultural family to receive cash from their property while continuing to live on and operate their farm or ranch.

The IRC Section 121 principal residence exclusion allows an individual to exclude up to $250,000 of taxable gain from the sale of a principal residence and a married couple filing a joint return to exclude up to $500,000 of gain.

CHAPTER 6

The Tax Reduction Wheel Of Fortune

A Financial Strategy For Selling A Farm Or Ranch

In this chapter we will illustrate a powerful wealth preservation strategy with the sale of a highly appreciated ranch. This strategy combines:

1. The IRC Section 1031 Exchange
2. The IRC Section 664 Charitable Remainder Trust
3. The IRC Section 121 Principal Residence Exclusion
4. Cash Sale
5. Joint and Survivor Life Insurance
6. An Irrevocable Life Insurance Trust

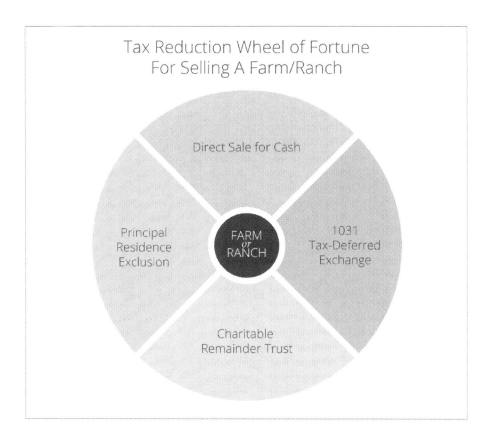

My friend, Jim Soft, former president of the Yellowstone Boys and Girls Ranch Foundation originally came up with the name Tax Reduction Wheel of Fortune while helping me present this strategy to a family in western Montana who was considering selling their ranch. The name was chosen because using the combination of financial tools in this illustration can save a fortune in taxes.

The illustration is of a highly appreciated $10 million ranch and involves the sale of land, livestock, machinery and equipment. It will examine how the use of proven wealth preservation strategies will allow a family to:

- Decrease taxes paid on the sale
- Increase annual income for retirement
- Increase wealth passed to heirs
- Increase money left to charitable organizations

Four sale scenarios are illustrated:

Option 1: Straight sale for cash of the entire $10 million ranch

Option 2: Straight sale for $5 million and 1031 exchange for $5 million

Option 3: Straight sale for $3 million, 1031 exchange for $3.5 million and charitable remainder trust for $3.5 million

Option 4: Straight sale for $3 million, 1031 exchange for $3.5 million, charitable remainder trust for $3.5 million and purchase of a $3.5 million second-to-die life insurance policy in an irrevocable life insurance trust.

Below is a summary of each of the four options. The pages that follow provide greater detail.

2015 Case Study Summary				
	Cash Sale	1031 Exchange & Cash Sale	1031, CRT & Cash Sale	1031, CRT, ILIT & Cash Sale
Federal and State Income Tax Liability	$2,284,600	$1,535,110	$488,571	$488,571
Annual Income from Reinvestment	$540,078	$592,542	$665,800	$570,800
To Charity Upon Second Death	$0	$0	$3,000,000	$3,000,000
Net Estate Passed to Heirs	$12,208,987	$14,976,623	$14,794,671	$16,971,887

	2015 Summary Schedule			
	Cash Sale	1031 Exchange & Cash Sale	1031, CRT & Cash Sale	1031, CRT, ILIT & Cash Sale
Total Tax Paid on Sale	$2,284,600	$1,535,110	$488,571	$488,571
Effective Tax Rate	22.85%	15.35%	7.69%	7.69%
Projected annual cash flow (before tax):				
Cash Investment 7%	$540,078	$347,542	$175,800	$175,800
1031 Investment 7%	-	245,000	245,000	245,000
CRT Investment 7%	-	-	245,000	245,000
Life Insurance				(95,000)
	$540,078	$592,542	$665,800	$570,800
Projected Net Estate to living heirs:				
Cash on Hand	$7,715,400	$4,964,890	$2,511,429	$2,511,429
Add'l Cash from reinvesting cash flow in excess of $200,000 per Year (23 yrs, less 35% tax/yr)	$5,392,912	6,610,437	8,310,509	6,105,870
Tax Savings From CRT - Charitable Contribution Carryover			450,135	450,135
1031 Exchange Property Future Value (2.5% annual appreciation)		6,145,712	6,145,712	6,145,712
ILIT Payout	-	-	-	3,500,000
	$13,108,312	$17,721,038	$17,417,785	$18,713,146
Amount to charity upon second death:				
CRT	$-	$-	$3,000,000	$3,000,000
Other donations	-	-	-	-
	$-	$-	$3,000,000	$3,000,000
Estate Tax Analyisis				
Value of Estate	$13,108,312	$17,721,038	$17,417,785	$18,713,146
Exclusion - Portability Married Couple	(10,860,000)	(10,860,000)	(10,860,000)	(10,860,000)
Exclusion - ILIT Proceeds				(3,500,000)
Taxable Estate	$2,248,312	$6,861,038	$6,557,785	$4,353,146
Estimated Estate Tax 40%	899,325	2,744,415	2,623,114	1,741,258
Net Estate left to heirs	$12,208,987	$14,976,623	$14,794,671	$16,971,887

The Tax Reduction Wheel Of Fortune | **101**

2015 - Cash Sale Sale Price $10,000,000					
Tax Analysis	Land	Building	Equipment & Livestock	Raised Livestock	Total
Sales Price Allocation	9,200,000	100,000	400,000	300,000	10,000,000
	92.00%	1.00%	4.00%	3.00%	
Original Cost	1,200,000	100,000	600,000	-	1,900,000
Accumulated Depreciation		100,000	600,000		700,000
Basis	1,200,000	-	-	-	1,200,000
Realized Gain/Loss	8,000,000	100,000	400,000	300,000	8,800,000
Recapture Gain/Loss		100,000	400,000	-	500,000
Capital Gain/Loss	8,000,000	-	-	300,000	8,300,000
	8,000,000	100,000	400,000	300,000	8,800,000
Projected Tax					
Federal:					
1245 Recapture Gain (39.6%)	-		158,400	-	158,400
1250 Recapture Gain (25%)		25,000	-		25,000
Long Term Capital Gain (20%)	1,600,000	-	-	60,000	1,660,000
Total Federal Tax	1,600,000	25,000	158,400	60,000	1,843,400
State:					
Recapture Rate (6.9%)	-	6,900	27,600		34,500
Capital Gain (4.9%)	392,000	-	-	14,700	406,700
Total State Tax	392,000	6,900	27,600	14,700	441,200
Total Tax Liability	1,992,000	31,900	186,000	74,700	2,284,600
Cash Flow					
Net Cash after Tax	7,208,000	68,100	214,000	225,300	7,715,400
Effective Tax Rate	22.85%				
Projected Annual Income (Cash Inv.)	540,078				
Total Annual Income	540,078				

2015 - 1031 Exchange
Sale Price $10,000,000

Tax Analysis	Land	Building	Equipment & Livestock	Raised Livestock	Total
Sales Price Allocation	9,200,000	100,000	400,000	300,000	10,000,000
	92.00%	1.00%	4.00%	3.00%	
Original Cost	1,200,000	100,000	600,000	-	1,900,000
Accumulated Depreciation	-	100,000	600,000	-	700,000
Basis	1,200,000	-	-	-	1,200,000
1031 Exchange	(3,500,000)		-	-	(3,500,000)
Realized Gain/Loss	4,990,000	100,000	400,000	300,000	5,790,000
Recapture Gain/Loss		100,000	400,000	-	500,000
Capital Gain/Loss	4,990,000	-	-	300,000	5,290,000
	4,990,000	100,000	400,000	300,000	5,790,000
Projected Tax					
Federal:					
1245 Recapture Gain (39.6%)	-	-	158,400	-	158,400
1250 Recapture Gain (25%)		25,000	-		25,000
Long Term Capital Gain (20%)	998,000	-	-	60,000	1,058,000
Total Federal Tax	998,000	25,000	158,400	60,000	1,241,400
State:					
Recapture Rate (6.9%)	-	6,900	27,600		34,500
Capital Gain (4.9%)	244,510	-	-	14,700	259,210
Total State Tax	244,510	6,900	27,600	14,700	293,710
Total Tax Liability	1,242,510	31,900	186,000	74,700	1,535,110
Cash Flow					
Net Cash after Tax	4,457,490	68,100	214,000	225,300	4,964,890
Effective Tax Rate	15.35%				
Projected Annual Income (Cash Inv.)	347,542				
Projected Annual Income (1031)	245,000				
Total Annual Income	592,542				

The Tax Reduction Wheel Of Fortune

2015 - 1031 Exchange and CRT
Sale Price $10,000,000

Tax Analysis	Land	Building	Equipment & Livestock	Raised Livestock	Total
Sales Price Allocation	9,200,000	100,000	400,000	300,000	10,000,000
	92.00%	1.00%	4.00%	3.00%	
Original Cost	1,200,000	100,000	600,000	-	1,900,000
Accumulated Depreciation	-	100,000	600,000	-	700,000
Basis	1,200,000	-	-	-	1,200,000
1031 Exchange	(3,500,000)		-	-	(3,500,000)
CRT	(3,500,000)				(3,500,000)
Realized Gain/Loss	1,913,000	100,000	400,000	300,000	2,713,000
Recapture Gain/Loss		100,000	400,000	-	500,000
Capital Gain/Loss	1,913,000	-	-	300,000	2,213,000
	1,913,000	100,000	400,000	300,000	2,713,000
Projected Tax					
Federal:					
1245 Recapture Gain (39.6%)			158,400	-	158,400
1250 Recapture Gain (25%)		25,000	-		25,000
Long Term Capital Gain (20%)	382,600	-	-	60,000	442,600
Total Federal Tax	382,600	25,000	158,400	60,000	626,000
State:					
Recapture Rate (6.9%)		6,900	27,600	-	34,500
Capital Gain (4.9%)	93,737	-	-	14,700	108,437
Total State Tax	93,737	6,900	27,600	14,700	142,937
Total Tax Liability	476,337	31,900	186,000	74,700	768,937
Charitable Deduction (limited 30% of AGI) Total $2,100,000 deduction *	313,900	100,000	400,000		813,900
Charitable Contribution (Tax Savings)					
Federal	47,085	25,000	158,400		230,485
State	15,381	6,900	27,600		49,881
Net Tax Liability	413,871	-	-	74,700	488,571
Cash Flow					
Net Cash after Tax	1,786,129	100,000	400,000	225,300	2,511,429
Effective Tax Rate	7.69%				
Projected Annual Income (Cash Inv.)	347,542				
Projected Annual Income (1031)	245,000				
Projected Annual Income (CRT)	245,000				
Total Annual Income	665,800				

* *$1,286,100 Charitable Contribution Carryover*

2015 - 1031 Exchange, CRT, and ILIT Sale Price $10,000,000					
Tax Analysis	Land	Building	Equipment & Livestock	Raised Livestock	Total
Sales Price Allocation	9,200,000	100,000	400,000	300,000	10,000,000
	92.00%	1.00%	4.00%	3.00%	
Original Cost	1,200,000	100,000	600,000	-	1,900,000
Accumulated Depreciation	-	100,000	600,000	-	700,000
Basis	1,200,000	-	-	-	1,200,000
1031 Exchange	(3,500,000)		-	-	(3,500,000)
CRT	(3,500,000)				(3,500,000)
Realized Gain/Loss	1,913,000	100,000	400,000	300,000	2,713,000
Recapture Gain/Loss		100,000	400,000	-	500,000
Capital Gain/Loss	1,913,000	-	-	300,000	2,213,000
	1,913,000	100,000	400,000	300,000	2,713,000
Projected Tax					
Federal:					
1245 Recapture Gain (39.6%)			158,400	-	158,400
1250 Recapture Gain (25%)		25,000	-		25,000
Long Term Capital Gain (20%)	382,600	-	-	60,000	442,600
Total Federal Tax	382,600	25,000	158,400	60,000	626,000
State:					
Recapture Rate (6.9%)		6,900	27,600	-	34,500
Capital Gain (4.9%)	93,737	-	-	14,700	108,437
Total State Tax	93,737	6,900	27,600	14,700	142,937
Total Tax Liability	476,337	31,900	186,000	74,700	768,937
Charitable Deduction (limited 30% of AGI) Total $2,100,000 deduction *	313,900	100,000	400,000		813,900
Charitable Contribution (Tax Savings)					
Federal	47,085	25,000	158,400		230,485
State	15,381	6,900	27,600		49,881
Net Tax Liability	413,871	-	-	74,700	488,571
Cash Flow					
Net Cash after Tax	1,786,129	100,000	400,000	225,300	2,511,429
Effective Tax Rate	7.69%				
Projected Annual Income (Cash Inv.)	347,542				
Projected Annual Income (1031)	245,000				
Projected Annual Income (CRT)	245,000				
Less: ILIT Premiums	(95,000)				
Total Annual Income	570,800				

$1,286,100 Charitable Contribution Carryover

The Tax Reduction Wheel Of Fortune

To request a similar analysis on the sale of your property, contact our office by calling 406-582-1264.

Summary

The Tax Reduction Wheel of Fortune is a powerful wealth preservation strategy that can be used with the sale of a highly appreciated farm or ranch. Combining the financial tools discussed in this chapter may enable a family to save a fortune in taxes, maximize retirement income and increase the amount of wealth passed to heirs and charitable organizations. Implementing this strategy requires careful planning in advance of a sale with an experienced team of professionals.

CHAPTER 7

Investing Cash Proceeds From The Sale

Part One

How you invest the proceeds from the sale of your farm or ranch will determine the retirement lifestyle you enjoy and the amount of wealth you pass to your heirs. This is not a decision to make lightly.

Just as it is important to get professional advice on strategies for saving taxes on the sale, it is also important to get professional advice on investing the sale proceeds. You have worked hard for your money, now it is time to make your money work hard for you.

In my experience, most farm and ranch families have little experience investing in assets outside their farm or ranch. Any profit they have made has typically been reinvested in their business. When they are faced with investing millions of dollars from the sale of their property, it can be very frightening. Many do not know where to start or who to trust. Consequently, some end up investing in what they know and are comfortable with which is typically land and CDs. While land can offer good appreciation potential, it typically offers a low cash flow return compared to other types of real estate and while CDs are safe from market risk, they expose investors to inflation risk and the risk of running out of money.

Getting Started

When deciding how to invest the cash proceeds from the sale of your farm or ranch, it is helpful to perform an assessment of your financial situation and determine what you want to achieve with your money going forward. This assessment should address factors such as your goals, your time horizon for investing, your tolerance for investment risk and your need for liquidity. Your answers to these questions should dictate how your money is invested.

Goals

The investment goal for most families who have sold their farm or ranch is to generate lifetime income and to leave an inheritance for their children and grandchildren – and to do so as tax efficiently as possible. Identifying your financial goals and the investment return required for attaining your goals is an important first step. Knowing the return you need to achieve your goals will help determine how you invest. Incorporating inflation into your analysis is an important and often neglected part of your goal planning analysis.

Time Horizon

Once you define your goals, next determine how long your money must work for you to achieve those goals. The time horizon for a particular investment will dictate the type of investment options you should consider. For example, if your investment time horizon is five years or less, you should not invest in the stock market. If you are investing for retirement, you typically want to plan for having enough money to last for your life expectancy. If you are age sixty-five and your life expectancy is age ninety, your time horizon for investing is twenty-five years. If you would like to leave an inheritance for your children or grandchildren, your time horizon for investing goes beyond your life expectancy.

Risk Tolerance

Assessing your tolerance for risk is imperative because if you invest in something that experiences a loss that is more than you can tolerate, you may be tempted to liquidate that investment at potentially the wrong time. One way to determine your tolerance for risk is to ask yourself what is the largest percentage loss (if any) you are willing to tolerate in a calendar year. Next, look at the historical performance of portfolios ranging from conservative to aggressive. Risk and return go together. You cannot achieve high returns without taking some investment risk.

When analyzing the historical performance of an investment, it is important to look at as many years as possible. A minimum time frame to look at is ten years. Any investment may have a good short-term track record but all investments go through up and down cycles. You want an investment that has proven itself over a long time. Having a good grasp on the amount of volatility you can tolerate with your investments will help you determine a portfolio that is suitable for you.

Liquidity

Another important consideration when investing is to determine your need for liquidity. Liquidity is the degree to which an asset can be bought or sold in the market without affecting the asset's price. Assets that can be easily bought or sold are known as liquid assets. Having adequate liquidity is important because if a need for cash arises and you do not have a ready source of liquid investments, you may have to sell an asset and for less than you could if you had more time.

Account Ownership

An important decision with respect to investing is choosing how to own the investment account. There are many ways you can own investments such as Individual, Joint Tenancy With Rights of Survivorship, Tenancy-In-Common, in different types of trusts, corporations or LLC's. How an account is owned can have serious tax and estate planning implications. It is critical to make sure your accounts are owned in a manner that lines up with your current needs and your estate planning objectives.

Taxable vs. Tax-Advantaged

The tax treatment of your investments is another important consideration. Not all accounts and investments are taxed the same. The types of products you own and the types of accounts you hold them in affect the taxes that you pay.

Real Return

Many families who sell their farm or ranch believe their only worry when it comes to investing is safety. What you should also be concerned about is being able to maintain your standard of living after inflation erodes your income in the years to come.

Real return is the annual percentage return realized on an investment, which is adjusted for changes in prices due to inflation and taxes. One of the main goals for most investors is to provide positive real returns – returns that outpace the rising cost of living. After all, if your investments are not outpacing inflation, you are going backwards in terms of your purchasing power. Taxes further reduce your return. To determine your real return, you should subtract both taxes and inflation. For example, if you earn five percent on a CD and your tax rate is thirty three percent and inflation is three and one half percent, your real return is zero.

CD or Money Market Rate	5%
Less Taxes @ 33%	3.35%
Less Inflation @ 3.35%	0%

Investing Sale Proceeds In CDs

Cash is the worst performing asset class in history. Over long periods of time, cash often generates a negative real return and has underperformed all other major asset classes. While cash (which includes CDs) are safe from market risk, they are not a risk-free investment. In fact, as you will learn in this chapter, they could be one of the riskiest investments to own.

I have asked families who have sold their farm or ranch and deposited all of the sale proceeds into CDs why they chose to do so. Their response is typically: "I need to know my money is safe." The irony is that while CDs are safe from market risk, they can expose you to one of the greatest risks you face which is either running out of money or facing an ever-decreasing standard of living. If you have enough money and you are not concerned about keeping up with inflation, CDs can work fine.

People often complain about how low CD interest rates are today compared to those of the past thirty-five years or so. When you look at the real returns of bank savings and CDs, however, you will discover that banks have never paid "good rates". People are just noticing it more today. CD rates, like all interest rates, track inflation. When inflation rates are high, interest rates are high and when inflation goes down, interest rates go down. In 1980, for example, when interest rates were 15%, inflation was 13%. So your real return in 1980 after taxes and inflation was close to what it is today.

Let's look at an example. If you had invested $1,000,000 in a one-year CD in 1981, your rate would have been 14.9% so you would have earned $149,000 of interest that year. By 1986 however, the rate dropped by more than half to 6.70% and by 2009, the rate dropped to

.88%. If you were living on the interest from this $1,000,000 CD, you would have seen your income drop from $149,000 per year to less than $10,000 per year. Not only did people see their incomes drop significantly during this time, but the cost of living greatly increased during this period. What cost $100,000 in 1981 cost approximately $230,600 in 2009.

You do not earn good returns in bank accounts because that is not what bank accounts are designed for. Bank accounts are designed for short-term cash reserves. CDs worked fine for your annual operating expenses on the farm or ranch but much better options exist for providing retirement income that outpaces inflation.

Real Returns Of Certificates Of Deposit vs. Stocks [1]

The chart on the next page compares the annual real return of CDs versus the S&P 500 stock index from 1985 to 2014. Taxes are not taken into consideration in this example. As you can see, the average inflation-adjusted return of the S&P 500 was 6.81% greater than CDs during this time frame.

CD Rates Compared With Stock Market Returns (1985–2014)					
Year	CD rate	S&P 500	Inflation	Real return of CDs	Real return of S&P 500
1985	8.54	31.73	3.79	4.58	26.92
1986	6.7	18.67	1.19	5.45	17.27
1987	7.21	5.25	4.33	2.76	0.88
1988	8.18	16.61	4.41	3.61	11.68
1989	9.46	31.69	4.64	4.61	25.85
1990	8.49	-3.1	6.25	2.11	-8.8
1991	6.06	30.47	2.98	2.99	26.69
1992	3.82	7.62	2.97	0.83	4.52
1993	3.34	10.08	2.81	0.52	7.07
1994	5.05	1.32	2.6	2.39	-1.25
1995	6.16	37.58	2.53	3.54	34.19
1996	5.61	22.96	3.38	2.16	18.94
1997	5.87	33.36	1.7	4.1	31.13
1998	5.58	28.58	1.61	3.91	26.54
1999	5.59	21.04	2.68	2.83	17.88
2000	6.79	-9.1	3.4	4 3.24	-12.12
2001	3.69	-11.89	1.6	2.06	-13.28
2002	1.81	-22.1	2.48	-0.65	-23.99
2003	1.23	28.68	2.04	-0.79	26.11
2004	1.75	10.88	3.34	-1.54	7.3
2005	3.79	4.91	3.34	0.44	1.52
2006	5.33	15.79	2.52	2.74	12.94
2007	5.35	5.49	4.11	1.19	1.33
2008	3.18	-37	-0.02	3.2	-36.99
2009	0.88	26.46	2.81	-1.88	23
2010	0.44	15.06	1.42	-0.97	13.45
2011	0.42	2.11	3.02	-2.52	-0.88
2012	0.44	16	1.76	-1.3	13.99
2013	0.27	32.39	1.51	-1.22	30.42
2014	0.43	13.69	0.66	-0.23	12.94
Average as of 12/31/14	4.35%	11.34%	2.72%	1.58%	8.39%

"Real return" is the gross return of CDs or the S&P 500 adjusted for inflation. While stocks incur more risk, certificates of deposit (CDs) offer a fixed rate of return, and the interest and principal on CDs will generally be insured by the FDIC up to $250,000. CD performance is based on average historical interest rates from Bloomberg. Data prior to 2013 is from Lipper. The Consumer Price Index (CPI) measures inflation. The S&P 500 Index is unmanaged and a common measurement of market performance. It is not possible to invest directly in an index. Past performance is not a guarantee of future results. Investments in mutual funds will fluctuate with market conditions, and you may have more or less than the original amount invested when you sell your shares.

Safety From Default Risk

The one thing I will tell you is the worst investment you can have is cash. Everybody is talking about cash being king and all that sort of thing. Cash is going to become worth less over time. But good businesses are going to become worth more over time.
– **Warren Buffett**

People typically invest in CDs because of the safety they feel it provides. By investing in bank CDs, you are essentially trying to protect yourself from default risk. Default risk is the risk that a company or individual will not be able to make the required payments on the money they owe you. Because of the FDIC insurance protection offered by banks, people feel they do not have to worry about their money if the bank goes broke.

The Federal Deposit Insurance Corporation (FDIC) is a U.S. government corporation that operates as an independent agency. As of January 2016, the FDIC provides deposit insurance guaranteeing the safety of a depositor's accounts in member banks up to $250,000 for each deposit ownership category in each insured bank. Although the FDIC is chartered by Congress, they do not receive any federal funding. Banks pay insurance premiums to the FDIC. If a bank goes bankrupt, they file a claim with the FDIC.

If you are concerned about protecting your money from default risk, a potentially better option is to invest in bonds issued by the U.S. federal government. The U.S. federal government doesn't just insure your money, it guarantees it. The guarantee printed on each bond issued by the government is a "full faith and credit obligation" of the government of the United States of America.

The U.S. government has the highest credit rating in the world and has never defaulted on an interest or principal payment. You might say, therefore, that it is the issuer of the world's safest investments. So, if you desire a safe investment, instead of a bank CD, consider investments backed by the full faith and credit of the U.S. federal government.

Certificates Of Deposit vs. Stock And Bond Mix

Investing in a portfolio of stock and bond mutual funds can potentially generate more retirement income than certificates of deposit. The charts on the next pages compare investing in CDs versus stocks and bonds with annual distributions made from each investment.

In these scenarios, one million dollars was deposited on January 1, 1994 into two accounts. Account one is represented by a three-month total return CD index. Account two is represented by an allocation of 60% to the S&P 500 stock index and 40% to the Barclays U.S. Aggregate Government Bond Index.

Annual withdrawals were made from each account. The first year withdrawal was $60,000 and these withdrawals were increased each year by the rate of inflation for that year. The stock and bond allocation was rebalanced at the beginning of each year to its 60/40 allocation. A summary of the results is provided on the next page.[2]

Scenario One: Certificates of Deposit				
Time Horizon	Beginning Value	Withdrawals	Ending Market Value	Return
1/1/94–12/31/94	$1,000,000.00	$60,000.00	$986,980.06	4.72%
1/1/95–12/31/95	$986,980.06	$61,563.12	$985,143.33	6.08%
1/1/96–12/31/96	$985,143.33	$63,567.17	$975,728.13	5.53%
1/1/97–12/31/97	$975,728.13	$64,729.53	$966,923.36	5.76%
1/1/98–12/31/98	$966,923.36	$65,731.56	$955,122.80	5.61%
1/1/99–12/31/99	$955,122.80	$67,455.13	$939,507.93	5.46%
1/1/00–12/31/00	$939,507.93	$69,779.80	$931,843.88	6.65%
1/1/01–12/31/01	$931,843.88	$71,102.54	$895,571.42	3.76%
1/1/02–12/31/02	$895,571.42	$72,665.63	$838,407.56	1.74%
1/1/03–12/31/03	$838,407.56	$73,948.15	$774,094.06	1.16%
1/1/04–12/31/04	$774,094.06	$76,553.49	$709,577.04	1.57%
1/1/05–12/31/05	$709,577.04	$79,198.74	$655,416.32	3.56%
1/1/06–12/31/06	$655,416.32	$80,761.92	$608,892.60	5.28%
1/1/07–12/31/07	$608,892.60	$84,239.80	$557,176.06	5.40%
1/1/08–12/31/08	$557,176.06	$85,140.81	$488,659.93	3.02%
1/1/09–12/31/09	$488,659.93	$86,705.93	$404,661.77	0.56%
1/1/10–12/31/10	$404,661.77	$87,697.13	$318,206.54	0.31%
1/1/11–12/31/11	$318,206.54	$90,673.67	$228,463.53	0.30%
1/1/12–12/31/12	$228,463.53	$92,273.28	$136,819.10	0.28%
1/1/13–12/31/13	$136,819.10	$93,414.81	$43,546.91 3	0.11%

Performance data quoted represents past performance. Past performance does not guarantee future results. The investment return and principal value of an investment will fluctuate so that an investor's shares, when redeemed, may be worth more or less than their original cost and current performance may be lower or higher than the performance quoted. For performance data current to the recent month end, please visit the Fund Families', Insurance Company, Stock, Closed End Fund or ETF Investor Websites or call them directly. Asset Class Performance returns do not reflect any management fees, transaction cost or expenses. Asset Classes and Indexes are unmanaged and one cannot invest directly in an Asset Class or Index The S&P 500 is a gauge of the large cap U.S. equities market. The index includes 500 leading companies in leading industries of the U.S. economy, capturing 75% coverage of U.S. equities. Reinvested assumes dividends are reinvested. Visit http://www.standardandpoors.com/indices for more information regarding Standard & Poor's indices.

Scenario Two: Balanced Stock And Bond Portfolio 60% S&P 500 Stock Index, 40% Barclays Aggregate Government Bond Index			
Time Horizon	Beginning Value	Withdrawals	Ending Market Value	Return
1/1/94–12/31/94	$1,000,000.00	$60,000.00	$931,654.70	-0.84%
1/1/95–12/31/95	$931,654.70	$61,563.12	$1,151,388.16	30.34%
1/1/96–12/31/96	$1,151,388.16	$63,567.17	$1,262,697.88	15.25%
1/1/97–12/31/97	$1,262,697.88	$64,729.53	$1,497,660.97	23.83%
1/1/98–12/31/98	$1,497,660.97	$65,731.56	$1,740,375.31	20.66%
1/1/99–12/31/99	$1,740,375.31	$67,455.13	$1,882,575.17	12.08%
1/1/00–12/31/00	$1,882,575.17	$69,779.80	$1,800,845.64	-0.64%
1/1/01–12/31/01	$1,800,845.64	$71,102.54	$1,665,712.04	-3.57%
1/1/02–12/31/02	$1,665,712.04	$72,665.63	$1,450,043.67	-8.62%
1/1/03–12/31/03	$1,450,043.67	$73,948.15	$1,640,955.71	18.34%
1/1/04–12/31/04	$1,640,955.71	$76,553.49	$1,693,674.07	7.91%
1/1/05–12/31/05	$1,693,674.07	$79,198.74	$1,681,695.73	3.98%
1/1/06–12/31/06	$1,681,695.73	$80,761.92	$1,788,399.41	11.19%
1/1/07–12/31/07	$1,788,399.41	$84,239.80	$1,820,227.63	6.51%
1/1/08–12/31/08	$1,820,227.63	$85,140.81	$1,391,113.01	-18.98%
1/1/09–12/31/09	$1,391,113.01	$86,705.93	$1,538,533.65	16.91%
1/1/10–12/31/10	$1,538,533.65	$87,697.13	$1,617,895.83	10.91%
1/1/11–12/31/11	$1,617,895.83	$90,673.67	$1,589,831.14	3.89%
1/1/12–12/31/12	$1,589,831.14	$92,273.28	$1,680,803.70	11.58%
1/1/13–12/31/13	$1,680,803.70	$93,414.81	$1,894,243.40	18.33%

Summary		
	Certificates of Deposit	Stocks and Bonds
Initial deposit	$1,000,000	$1,000,000
Initial annual withdrawal	$60,000	$60,000
Total withdrawals	$1,527,202.19	$1,527,202.19
Ending value	$43,546.91	$1,894,243.40
Average Annualized Return	4.29%	8.95%
Cumulative return	131.94%	455.58%

In the above illustrations, the CD's nearly ran out of money in the 20th year while the stocks and bonds had an ending value of $1,894,243.40.

It is worth noting that two of the worst historical periods for U.S. stocks occurred during this time frame. While past performance is not a predictor of future performance, this analysis presents strong reasons to consider investing in the stock and bond market versus CDs.

Segregating Accounts For Parents And Children

Agricultural families often have two goals when investing proceeds from the sale of their farm or ranch. One goal is to provide for retirement income for the parents. The other goal is to provide an inheritance for their children and grandchildren. Rather than investing in one portfolio for both goals, a prudent strategy may be to create two (or more) portfolios. The parent's portfolio is invested conservatively and the children's (and grandchildren's) portfolios are invested more aggressively. The premise behind this strategy is if your time horizon for investing is longer, you are able to ride out the up and down cycles of a more aggressively allocated portfolio which should over time, produce higher returns.

Balancing Risk And Reward

Since 1926, the U.S. stock market has grown at an average annual rate of approximately 10% per year. Unfortunately, the stock market doesn't go up each year in a straight line. There can be large variations in returns from year to year. While the U.S. stock market has averaged around 10% annually over the long term, historically it has yielded negative returns about 25% of the time.

If you want to earn positive real returns over time, you may need to own some stocks and embrace some volatility in returns. Without an understanding of how markets work, you will likely fall prey to the common mistakes investors make.

One strategy to reduce the volatility of stocks, is to add bonds to a portfolio. Balancing the percentage of stocks and bonds you own in your portfolio is a way to adjust your level of risk and reward. The graph on the next page shows long-term average annual returns for various asset allocations between U.S. stocks and bonds, and the number of years the allocations incurred a loss. [3]

Asset Allocation	Average Annual Returns 1926-2015	Number of Years With a Loss
100% cash	3.48%	1 of 90
100% bonds	5.40%	14 of 90
80% bonds, 20% stocks	6.70%	12 of 90
70% bonds, 30% stocks	7.28%	13 of 90
60% bonds, 40% stocks	7.82%	14 of 90
50% bonds, 50% stocks	8.32%	17 of 90
40% bonds, 60% stocks	8.77%	20 of 90
30% bonds, 70% stocks	9.18%	21 of 90
20% bonds, 80% stocks	9.54%	23 of 90
100% stocks	10.13%	25 of 90

Past performance is no guarantee of future returns. The performance of an index is not an exact representation of any particular investments, as you cannot invest directly in an index. There is no guarantee that any particular asset allocation or mix of funds will meet your investment objectives or provide you with a given level of income. When determining which index to use and for what period, we selected the index that we deemed to be a fair representation of the characteristics of the referenced market, given the information currently available. For U.S. stock market returns, we used the Standard and Poor's 90 index from 1926 to March 3, 1957' the S&P 500 Index from March 4, 1957, through 1974; The Dow Jones Wilshire 5000 Index from 1975 to April 22, 2005; the MSCI US Broad Market Index from April 23, 2005, to June 2, 2013; and the CRSP US Total Market Index thereafter. For U.S. bond market returns, we used the S&P High Grade Corporate Index from 1926 through 1968, the Citigroup High Grade Index from 1969 through 1972, the Lehman Brothers U.S. Long Credit AA Index from 1973through 1975, the Barclays U.S. Aggregate Bond Index from 1976 through 2009, and the Barclays U.S. Aggregate Float Adjusted Index thereafter. For U.S. short-term returns, we used the Ibbotson U.S. 30-Day Treasury Bill Index from 1926 through 1977 and the Citigroup 3-Month U.S. Treasury Bill Index thereafter.

Taxation Of Stocks vs. Certificates Of Deposit

Not only do stocks and bonds offer greater growth potential over CDs, they also offer tax advantages over CDs. Some of these advantages include:

- Gains in stocks grow tax-deferred. The gains are only taxed when they are realized – the stocks are sold. Interest income from CDs is taxed each year.
- Taxes due on the sale of stocks and bonds held for more than one year pay capital gain tax rates, which in 2016, have a maximum rate of 23.8%. Interest income from a CD is taxed at ordinary income tax rates, which in 2016 have a maximum rate of 39.6%. Much of the dividend income from stocks is also taxed at the lower rates.
- Stocks receive a stepped-up cost basis at death. Thus, if one holds appreciated stocks or stock mutual funds until death, heirs could sell the appreciated shares for current market value and avoid paying income tax on the gains.

How To Invest In The Stock And Bond Market

Unfortunately, the financial media, Wall Street and the investment brokerage industry disseminate information on investing that is often designed to entertain, to sell advertising and to move money so they can generate fees and commissions. Once you understand how destructive listening to much of their advice can be, you will learn to ignore much of what you hear from the media and Wall Street.

Another source of investment information comes from academia. Academia refers to the people and institutions dedicated to the activities of teaching and learning, including research and discovery. This would include schools, colleges and universities.

Over the past sixty years, academic research has discovered and established the most effective ways to invest. By following the guidelines outlined in this chapter and chapter eight, you can benefit from their research.

Active vs. Passive

While there are many strategies for investing in the stock and bond market, they all boil down to two basic investment philosophies; active management and passive management. Active management attempts to "beat the market" through a variety of techniques such as stock picking, sector rotation and marketing timing. In contrast, passive money managers avoid speculation and subjective forecasting. They take a longer-term view and attempt to deliver market returns using index or asset class funds.

Active management assumes the market is not completely efficient — that some securities are over-or underpriced and that it is possible to figure out which ones they are. On the other hand, passive investment managers avoid speculation and attempt to capture the market's returns by investing in index funds without regard for future forecasts.

To a large extent, the investment media and brokerage industry would like you to believe that the key to successful investing is picking the right stocks, sectors or asset classes and getting in and out of those stocks, sectors or asset classes at the right times. Wall Street and the brokerage industry try to create the impression that their superior investment insight and ability to pick stocks, sectors and time the market will help you attain better performance.

A 2008 study by Dartmouth finance professor Kenneth French estimated investors in the U.S. pay roughly $100 billion per year in fees and other expenses in an attempt to "beat the market" rather than investing in low-fee index funds that track the broader performance of the stock market [4].

Another study by Kenneth French and the 2013 Nobel Prize in Economics winner Eugene Fama determined only one percent of active managers outperformed the market due to skill [5].

Can Active Money Managers Outperform The Market?

Many people are under the false notion that in order to be a successful stock market investor you need to hire someone who is continually monitoring the market and who will use their superior insight, knowledge, resources and abilities to get in and out of the right stocks and/or investment sectors at the right times. It assumes you need to be able to forecast what will happen in the economy and accurately predict the market's direction in advance.

Active money managers try to sell you on their superior stock picking and market timing ability to justify the higher fees they charge. The measure of successful active management lies in the ability of a manager to deliver above-average returns consistently over multiple years. Demonstrating the ability to outperform repeatedly is the only proven way to differentiate a manager's luck from skill.

A comprehensive study was performed to determine the percentage of actively managed mutual funds that outperformed their passive index benchmark. From January 1st of 2000 through December, 31st of 2015, of the mutual funds that survived this period of time, only 17% of stock funds beat their benchmark index and only 7% of bond funds beat their benchmark index.[6] The results of this study demonstrate how difficult it is to beat the market using active management and why more and more people are turning to passive index fund investment strategies.

The idea that you need to hire an investment guru to have a positive investment experience is simply not true. You can have a successful experience investing in the stock market without working with such an individual. In fact, by investing in the right mix of index or asset class funds and avoiding emotional reactions to the market, you will likely beat the vast majority of active money managers over time.

Stock Picking

Stock picking is the attempt to pick winning stocks – stocks that will outperform the market. Many people either attempt to pick stocks themselves or they hire money managers to pick stocks for them.

If you invest in an actively managed mutual fund, the manager of the fund attempts to outperform their index benchmark by buying and selling stocks that he or she believes will do better than the market. As you've seen in the previous study, the odds of active money managers outperforming their index benchmark are very small.

To illustrate how difficult it is to pick winning stocks, consider this. From 1994 – 2015, only the top-performing 25% of stocks from around the world were responsible for the market gains during this timeframe. The remaining 75% of the stocks in the total market database collectively generated a loss of 5.4%. [7]

A logical question one might ask is: if a small percentage of stocks often accounts for the majority of the market's long-term returns, why not just invest in these top-performing stocks? Unfortunately, it is not that easy. A portfolio of the most carefully chosen stocks can easily end up with none of the best-performing stocks in the future and could easily produce negative returns for many years. The only way you can be assured of owning the best-performing stocks of each country in the future is to own the entire market.

Market Timing

> "There are three kinds of people who make market predictions. Those that don't know, those who don't know what they don't know, and those who know darn well they don't know but get paid big bucks for pretending to know." — Burton Malkiel (Author of the best-selling book, A Random Walk Down Wall Street)

Market timing is an attempt to avoid stock market losses by being invested in the market when the market is going up and being in cash when the market is going down. While attempting to time the market may seem like a smart thing to do, it is very difficult and frequently very costly. In fact, attempting to time the market can be devastating to your long-term investment performance. According to a recent 10-year study by Morningstar, investors are losing an average of about 2.5 percent per year to poor market timing decisions. [8]

Another market timing study looked at the impact of missing a few of the best days in the market. This study showed how $1,000 invested in the S&P 500 index from 1970 to 2015 grew to $89,678, an annualized compound return of 10.27 percent. The study further revealed that if you missed the 25 days with the biggest gains during this 45-year period, you would have only accumulated $21,224. [9]

Unfortunately, many financial advisors attempt to move your money in and out of the market to enhance returns. These advisors know they cannot time the market but the success of their business largely depends on having you believe they can. It is easy to attract clients by telling them you can get the upward benefits of the market without downside risk. If you're talking to an advisor who claims they can successfully time the market, I suggest you find another advisor.

Stock market gains and declines are often concentrated in a small number of days each year. Missing just a few days can have a dramatic impact on returns. Stock and bond prices fluctuate in value and you must accept that when you invest. While it can be scary listening to the media, you must learn to resist the urge to sell when the market is going down.

Focus On The Boy, Not The Yo-Yo

People who invest in the stock market often focus on the wrong thing – they focus on the daily up and down movement of the stocks prices versus the upward movement of the market over time.

People fear the stock market because stock prices are volatile and they can see when their money goes down. By focusing on the daily ups and downs of the market, people can lose sight of the fact that stocks have historically gone up more than they have gone down and over time, the market has gone up.

Here is an illustration that may help you learn to shift your focus. Imagine a boy walking up a hill playing with a yo-yo. If you focus on the yo-yo, you'll be obsessed with its constant up and down movements while ignoring the fact that the boy is steadily climbing higher. So it is with the stock market. Don't focus on the yo-yo, focus on the fact that the market has steadily climbed over time.

Mutual Funds And Exchange Traded Funds

Mutual funds and exchange traded funds (ETFs) are the preferred method for investing in the stock and bond market today. Mutual funds and ETFs offer several advantages:

- The first advantage, and this is a big one, is diversification.

You can own hundreds and thousands of individual stocks or bonds in a single mutual fund or ETF. This significantly reduces your risk of holding a small number of individual securities.

- A second reason is convenience. It is far easier to own a properly diversified portfolio of stocks and bonds through a mutual fund or ETF than it is to purchase hundreds or thousands of individual stocks and bonds.

- Third, the trading costs of buying and selling individual stocks and bonds are often prohibitively high for individual investors. So high-priced in fact, that gains made from the stock's price appreciation can easily be wiped out by the costs of selling shares of the stock. With a mutual fund or ETF, the cost of trades are spread over all investors in the fund, thereby lowering the cost per individual. And, the operating cost of mutual funds and exchange-traded funds (known as the Expense Ratio) have gone down considerably over time. Today, you can buy an index fund that owns thousands of stocks with an expense ratio as low as .10%.

- Automatic rebalancing without incurring costs. You can now purchase mutual funds that own thousands of securities all over the world. Many of these funds automatically rebalance the holdings in the fund on a regular basis. Because the rebalancing is done within the fund, you do not incur capital gain taxes or transaction costs for the trades that are placed. Trying to maintain a target allocation to hundreds of individual stocks and bonds would be very costly and time-consuming.

Index Funds

An index fund is a type of mutual fund with a portfolio constructed to match or track the components of a market index, such as the Standard & Poor's 500 Index (S&P 500). Index funds have become the preferred method of investing for millions of investors. They have risen from just three percent of the market in 1993 to more than thirty percent in 2014. [10] Index funds do not engage in the tactics of stock picking and market timing. Rather, index fund managers simply buy and hold the securities within an index. Companies are purchased and held within the index when they meet the index parameters. Stocks are sold when they move outside of these parameters and no longer meet the index rules of construction.

You cannot invest directly in an index; you can, however, invest in a mutual fund that holds the securities that comprise an index. There are indexes that represent just about every segment of the stock and bond market you can imagine. The S&P 500 stock index is the most well-known index. It is composed of 500 large U.S. companies and represents approximately 75% of the U.S. stock market capitalization. When you hear that a portfolio has "beaten the market" it is likely being compared with the S&P 500.

Index funds are preferred over active investing for many reasons. First, active management costs more. The average expense ratio of active managed mutual funds is typically four to five times higher than the average expense ratio of index funds. Second, active trading of securities reduces returns due to transaction costs. Third, active management generates more taxes. Fourth, most active managed funds hold more cash than index funds, which reduces the returns over time and fifth, active traders make many of the same mistakes discussed in this chapter that individual investors make.

Asset Class Funds

Asset class funds offer an investment approach similar to index funds with distinct advantages. With asset class investing, mutual fund managers have flexibility with buying and selling securities. This trading flexibility can greatly enhance the efficiency of the fund. The asset class fund managers can choose investments from the entire universe of securities in an asset class — not just the ones included in an index list. And, the managers can assign a weighting to the security in the fund based on the company's size, price and profitability rather than the company's market capitalization.

For example, stock indexes such as the S&P 500 weight companies in the index based upon the company's market capitalization. This gives a higher weighting to large growth companies within the index. Research has shown, however, that small companies outperform large companies over time and value companies outperform growth companies over time. Asset class mutual funds offered through some mutual fund companies offer the ability for an investor to own a diversified portfolio of securities, similar to an index fund, but with higher weightings to small and value companies as well as highly profitable companies.

To help you understand this weighting of investment holdings concept, think of a mutual fund as an ice cube tray with each cube representing a company and the amount you own of each company is represented by the amount of water in the cube. By tilting the ice cube tray one way or another, you determine how much water is in each cube (company). Traditional index funds have more water in large growth companies. Asset class funds tilt the ice cube tray so more water is in small companies, value companies, and highly profitable companies relative to traditional index funds.

Asset class fund managers can also exclude initial public offerings (IPOs), financially distressed and bankrupt companies and illiquid stocks that do not truly represent the class. In addition, the managers can draw from a wider universe of securities. For example, while there are over 3,000 small-cap stocks in the U.S. to choose from, most small-cap index funds and ETFs limit themselves to the 2,000 small-cap stocks of the Russell 2000.

Because asset class funds aren't tied to an index, managers have the flexibility to decide when to add a security to the fund. That means managers aren't forced to buy a stock the day it becomes part of an index — when its price is likely to be high. Instead they trade carefully and patiently in an effort to minimize transaction costs. They are also free to capitalize on block trading and securities lending whenever possible. Independence from index tracking generally means lower trading costs.

Advice From Warren Buffet

Warren Buffet is widely regarded as one of the greatest investors of all time. He has a tremendous record of picking winning stocks. What does this legendary investor say about how to invest?

In the 2013 annual letter to Berkshire shareholders, Warren Buffet instructed his heirs to invest in index funds. Buffet went on to say:

> "I have good news for the non-investment professionals: The typical investor doesn't need this skill. In aggregate, American business has done wonderfully over time and will continue to do so (though, most assuredly, in unpredictable fits and starts). In the 20th Century, the Dow Jones Industrials index advanced from 66 to 11,497, paying a rising stream of dividends to boot.

> The 21st Century will witness further gains, almost certain to be substantial. The goal of the non-professional should not be to pick winners – neither he nor his "helpers" can do that – but should rather be to own a cross-section of businesses that in aggregate are bound to do well."

Again, from the letter:

> "Both individuals and institutions will constantly be urged to be active by those who profit from giving advice or effecting transactions. The resulting frictional costs can be huge and, for investors in aggregate, devoid of benefit. So ignore the chatter, keep your costs minimal, and invest in stocks as you would in a farm. There might be bad weather. There could be a crop failure one year or the next. There are certain costs of doing business, mostly predictable and best kept low. And, largely, there's nothing to do. Like crops in the field, a long-term, mostly stock investment cannot help but produce a reasonable return — assuming you don't overthink it and don't spend willy-nilly in a vain attempt to make it grow faster."

Buffett himself owns a 400-acre farm. Has he laid awake at night worrying about fluctuations in the farm's market price? No, says Buffett, he has focused on its long-term value. And he counsels investors to take the same relaxed approach to liquid investments such as shares of stock as they do to the value of their family farm.

"Those people who can sit quietly for decades when they own a farm or apartment house too often become frenetic when they are exposed to a stream of stock quotations," Buffett said. "For these investors, liquidity is transformed from the unqualified benefit it should be to a curse."

"Owners of stocks . . . too often let the capricious and irrational behavior of their fellow owners cause them to behave irrationally," Buffett says. "Because there is so much chatter about markets, the economy, interest rates, price behavior of stocks, etc., some investors believe it is important to listen to pundits—and, worse yet, important to consider acting upon their comments."

CHAPTER 8

Investing Cash Proceeds From The Sale

Part Two

Asset Allocation

Asset allocation is the process of dividing your investment dollars among different asset classes. An asset class is a group of securities that exhibit similar characteristics, behave similarly in the marketplace, and are subject to the same laws and regulations. The five main asset classes are equities (stocks), fixed-income (bonds), cash equivalents (CD's and money market instruments), real estate and commodities.

These five main asset classes are broken down further by a variety of classifications. For example, with stocks you can choose to invest in U.S. companies, international companies, large companies, small companies, growth companies, value companies etc. With bonds, you can choose to invest in corporate bonds, government bonds, municipal bonds, high credit quality bonds, low credit quality bonds, short-term maturities or long-term maturities.

Asset classes are the building blocks of an investment portfolio. The asset classes you choose to invest in will largely determine the investment performance you receive. While Wall Street likes you to believe that investment performance is mainly due to a manager's ability to pick stocks and time the market, research has proven otherwise. A landmark study published in the Financial Analyst Journal in May of 1991 revealed that asset allocation accounted for over 90% of portfolio performance with less than 10% of performance due to the ability to pick stocks or time the market. [11] A more recent study by The Vanguard Group in 2013 had similar findings. [12] Their study concluded that 88% of portfolio performance is due to asset allocation. In other words, the asset classes you choose to invest in and the percentage of your portfolio that you allocate to each asset class will likely have a greater impact on your portfolio's return than anything else.

Effective Diversification

The best single piece of advice I have for investors is to diversify, diversify, diversify. Everyone has heard the saying, "Don't put all your eggs in one basket". Not everyone, however, understands the difference between effective and ineffective diversification. Effective diversification combines multiple asset classes that have low correlation with each other. By combining asset classes with low correlation, you can potentially smooth out the large swings in volatility of a portfolio that contains one asset class. Effective diversification enables investors to potentially reduce the overall risk in their portfolios and increase their long-term potential returns.

Most stocks within an asset class tend to go up or down at the same time. To be effectively diversified, you need to own multiple asset classes. An example of ineffective diversification occurred during the days of the tech-bubble (also referred to as the dot-com boom). This was a historic speculative bubble covering roughly 1997–2000. Many people during this time frame thought they were diversified because they owned multiple technology stocks and/or technology stock funds. When the tech bubble burst though, most tech stocks went down drastically.

The Asset Class Performance Chart on the next pages illustrates how all asset classes go through up and down cycles. Each column contains colored boxes representing ten different asset classes. The top performing asset class each year is ranked at the top of the chart and the worst performing asset class is at the bottom.

As you can see, there is random movement of each asset class over time. The best performing asset class in one year is often the worst or close to the worst performing asset class the next year. Many investors tend to pick their investments based upon the recent performance of that investment. This is another common reason many investors are frustrated with the results they achieve.

Smart Diversification Can Help You Stay on Track [13]
Asset Class Performance Percentage 2001-2015

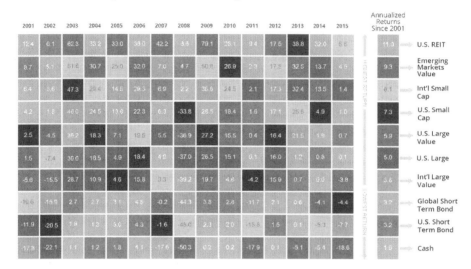

Diversification does not guarantee a profit or protect against a loss.
Source: Morningstar Direct 2015. Index representation as follows: U.S. Large Cap (S&P 500 Index), U.S. Large Value (Russell 1000 Value TR Index), U.S. Small Cap (Russell 2000 TR Index), U.S. REIT (Dow Jones U.S. Select REIT TR Index), International Large Value (MSCI World Ex USA Value Index (net div.)), International Small Cap (MSCI World Ex USA Small Cap (net div.)), Emerging Markets Value (MSCI Emerging Markets Value Index (net div)), Global Short Term Bond (Citi WGBI 1-5Yr Hdg USD), U.S. Short Term Bond (BofA ML Corp & Govt 1-3 Yr TR).,Indexes are unmanaged baskets of securities that are not available for direct investment by investors. Index performance does not reflect the expenses associated with the management of an actual portfolio. Treasury notes are guaranteed as to repayment of principal and interest by the U.S. government. Past performance is not a guarantee of future results. All investments involve risk, including loss of principal. Foreign securities involve additional risks, including foreign currency changes, political risks, foreign taxes, and different methods of accounting and financial reporting. Fixed income investments are subject to interest rate and credit risk. Emerging markets involve additional risks, including, but not limited to, currency fluctuation, political instability, foreign taxes, and different methods of accounting and financial reporting. Real estate securities funds are subject to changes in economic conditions, credit risk and interest rate fluctuations. All investments involve risk, including the loss of principal and cannot be guaranteed against loss by a bank, custodian, or any other financial institution. © 2016 LWI Financial Inc. ("Loring Ward") is an investment advisor registered with the Securities and Exchange Commission. Securities transactions are offered through its affiliate, Loring Ward Securities Inc., member FINRA/SIPC. B 15-012 (Exp. 03/2017)

Standard Deviation And The Impact Of Volatility On Returns

Standard deviation is a very important element of investing. In finance, standard deviation is applied to the annual rate of return of an investment to measure the investment's volatility. The higher an investment's standard deviation, the higher its volatility.

The volatility of a portfolio has a big impact on the amount of money you accumulate or distribute for retirement. You can have two portfolios with the same average annual return but the portfolio with lower volatility will have more money. In the chart below, both portfolios started with an initial deposit of $100,000 and both have an average return of ten percent. As you can see, however, the portfolio with lower volatility has a higher ending value.

Year	Low Volatility		High Volatility	
	Growth of $100,000	Annual Return	Growth of $100,000	Annual Return
1	$110,000	10.00%	34%	$134,000
2	$115,500	5.00%	-9%	$121,940
3	$131,670	14.00%	26%	$153,644
4	$143,520	9.00%	-16%	$129,061
5	$162,178	13.00%	31%	$169,070
6	$165,421	2.00%	-1.00%	$167,380
7	$185,272	12.00%	18.00%	$197,508
8	$214,916	16.00%	-12%	$173,807
9	$227,811	6.00%	21.00%	$210,306
10	$257,426	13.00%	8.00%	$227,313
Average Return		10.00%		10.00%
Compound Return		9.90%		8.50%
Standard Deviation		4.50%		18.60%

Hypothetical portfolios for illustrative purposes only. Diversification does not assure a profit or protect against a loss.

Don't Stop At The S&P 500

You might conclude from reading thus far that all you have to do is invest in an S&P 500 index fund. While it is true that the S&P 500 index has outperformed the vast majority of large U.S. stock mutual funds and has performed very well historically, you can potentially do better by adding other asset classes to your portfolio.

The S&P 500 represents large U.S. stocks. An effectively diversified portfolio should include stocks, bonds and real estate from all around the world and it should include small companies as well as large companies and value companies as well as growth companies.

The "Lost Decade"

To illustrate why your portfolio should contain other asset classes besides the S&P 500, let's look at the performance of several asset classes from the last decade. The years 2001 – 2010 are referred to as the "Lost Decade". That's because during this time frame, large U.S. stocks, as represented by the S&P 500, actually lost money.

As you can see in the chart on the next page[14], while U.S. large stocks returned nothing from 2001 through 2010, other asset classes performed far better during this time period. This is a great example of why you should own multiple asset classes in your portfolio.

10-Year Index Returns: January 2001 – December 2010	
U.S. Large Cap Stocks	0%
U.S. Mid Cap Stocks	64.73%
U.S. Small Cap Stocks	78.76%
International Developed Market Stocks	134.39%
Bonds	175.73%
Real Estate	228.19%
Emerging Markets Stocks	437.00%

Investing Internationally

Investors often tend to invest in what they know and are comfortable with. This holds true for investing in one's own country. Many of the people I meet with often have their entire portfolio invested in U.S. companies. While it may feel more secure to invest in your own country, you are missing out on potential opportunities by limiting your investing to the U.S. Just as investing in one company or one industry carries more risk than investing in a broad mix of companies and industries, investing in just one country carries more risk than investing in multiple countries.

Market Capitalization Of Global Stock Markets

To help you understand the opportunities available for investing internationally, let's take a look at the market capitalization of global stock markets. A country's equity market capitalization, or market cap, reflects the total value of shares issued by all publicly traded companies and is calculated as share price times the number of shares outstanding. The chart below shows the global market cap as of December 31, 2015. [15]

	Number of Countries	Number of Stocks	Total Value	Weight
US	1	3,021	22.10 Trillion	53.16%
Developed Markets ex US	22	3,442	15.44 Trillion	37.14%
Emerging Markets	23	2,719	4.03 Trillion	9.70%
Total	46	9,182	41.57 Trillion	100%

Over the last few decades, we have seen a large shift in the relative stock market capitalization of the world. While the U.S. remains the largest country by market capitalization, the growth of international investments has been significant and is expected to continue. This is not because the U.S. economy is not growing or will continue to grow, but rather because international and emerging markets are growing faster.

Ranking Of Markets Around The World

As you can see in the chart below titled: Ranking of Markets Around the World [16], for the ten-year period ending December 31, 2014, the United States ranked 22nd out of 45 countries in terms of annualized returns in U.S. dollars. This is another example of why your portfolio should contain investments in countries other than the U.S.

Ranking of Markets Around the World
Ten-Year Performance in US Dollars
Annualized Returns Year Ending December 31, 2014

1. Philippines	16. Korea	31. New Zealand
2. Peru	17. Switzerland	32. UK
3. Colombia	18. Australia	33. Spain
4. Indonesia	19. Turkey	34. Finland
5. Egypt	20. Sweden	35. Poland
6. China	21. Canada	36. France
7. Thailand	22. USA	37. Belgium
8. Denmark	23. Morocco	38. Japan
9. India	24. Chile	39. Russia
10. Mexico	25. Germany	40. Italy
11. Malaysia	26. Netherlands	41. Hungary
12. Singapore	27. Taiwan	42. Portugal
13. Brazil	28. Israel	43. Austria
14. Hong Kong	29. Czech Republic	44. Ireland
15. South Africa	30. Norway	45. Greece

Randomness Of U.S. vs. International Returns

The year-by-year returns of world markets vary widely as seen in the table on the next page. It is impossible to predict from year-to-year which country or countries will perform best and no one knows from year-to-year if the U.S market will outperform the international market or vice versa. To capture the returns of top performing countries each year, it is important to diversify globally. We recommend diversifying among domestic, and international developed and emerging markets. The potential diversification benefits of international investing are stronger when you include international small companies and emerging market securities because their prices are typically more closely related to their local economies than to the global economy. In contrast, large international companies that have operations all over the world typically have a high correlation with large U.S. based companies.

Randomness of Returns
1999-2014

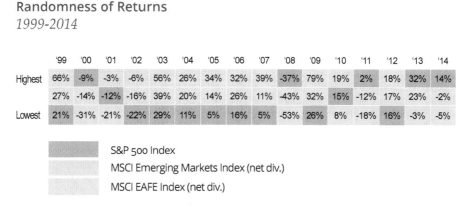

Source: Morningstar Direct 2015

What Is The Right Mix Of U.S. And Non-U.S. Securities?

Research dating back to 1972 has shown that by combining U.S. and international stocks in a portfolio, an investor is able to increase returns and lower the standard deviation of the portfolio. From 1972 – 2014, a portfolio allocated roughly 60% to the U.S. equities and 40% to international equities achieved the optimum balance of risk and return. [18]

U.S. Large represented by the S&P 500 Index, International Large represented by the MSCI EAFE Index (gross dividends).

Factors That Determine Performance

Academic research has identified three factors that account for almost all of the performance of stocks. [19] These three factors of returns are:

1. Size Factor: Large vs. Small companies
2. Price Factor: Value vs. Growth companies
3. Profitability Factor: Highly profitable vs. Low profitable companies

As you can see in the chart on the next page, research has shown that small companies have historically outperformed large companies over time, value companies have historically outperformed growth companies over time and highly profitable companies have historically outperformed less profitable companies over time. This holds true for not only U.S. stocks but stocks from all over the world. [20]

Dimensions of Expected Returns
Historical premiums and returns (annualized): US, Developed ex US, and Emerging Markets

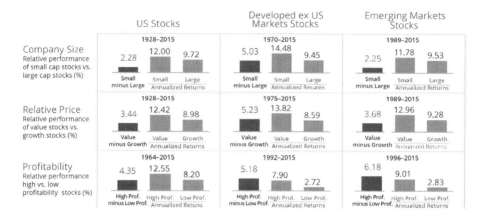

Information provided by Dimensional Fund Advisors LP.

In USD. US size premium: Dimensional US Small Cap Index minus S&P 500 Index. US relative price premium: Fama/French US Value Index minus Fama/French US Growth Index. US profitability premium: Dimensional US High Profitability Index minus Dimensional US Low Profitability Index. Dev. ex US size premium: Dimensional Intl. Small Cap Index minus MSCI World ex USA Index (gross div.). Dev. ex US relative price premium: Fama/French International Value index minus Fama/French International Growth Index. Dev. ex US profitability premium: Dimensional International High Profitability Index minus Dimensional International Low Profitability Index. Emerging Markets size premium: Dimensional Emerging Markets Small Cap Index minus MSCI Emerging Markets Index (gross div.). Emerging Markets relative price premium: Fama/French Emerging Markets Value Index minus Fama/French Emerging Markets Growth Index. Emerging Markets profitability premium: Dimensional Emerging Markets High Profitability Index minus Dimensional Emerging Markets Low Profitability Index. Profitability is measured as operating income before depreciation and amortization minus interest expense scaled by book. Indices are not available for direct investment. Their performance does not reflect the expenses associated with the management of an actual portfolio. Past performance is not a guarantee of future results. Index returns are not representative of actual portfolios and do not reflect costs and fees associated with an actual investment. Actual returns may be lower. See "Index Descriptions" for descriptions of Dimensional and Fama/French index data. Eugene Fama and Ken French are members of the Board of Directors for and provide consulting services to Dimensional Fund Advisors LP. The S&P data is provided by Standard & Poor's Index Services Group. MSCI data © MSCI 2016, all rights reserved.

Structuring a portfolio with higher weightings to small, value and highly profitable companies is a way that investors can seek to receive higher returns over long periods of time. Dimensional Fund Advisors (DFA), one of the world's largest mutual fund companies, offer mutual funds that are similar to index funds. The DFA funds allow an investor to efficiently capture the returns of the total U.S and International stock markets while providing increased exposure to these three factors of returns.

Investing In Bonds

Bonds are loans you make to a government, government agency, or corporation to finance various projects and other needs. The issuer of the bond agrees to repay you at a fixed interest rate by a specified date, or maturity. Bond prices are much less volatile than stock prices and they often move in the opposite direction of stocks. Therefore, bonds often provide stability to counter balance the high volatility of stocks.

You can invest in individual bonds or in bond mutual funds or exchange traded funds. There are several advantages of investing in bond funds versus individual bonds. Two of the major factors are diversification and convenience.

Diversification is important for bonds, as it is for all asset classes and bond funds allow broad diversification at a very low cost. Bond funds are simpler and more convenient than individual bonds because investors in a bond fund can buy or sell additional shares at any time in any quantity and there is usually no transaction fee for buying or selling additional shares. It is also generally simpler to have bond funds automatically reinvest dividends and then just sell a fixed amount of the fund on a monthly or quarterly basis to provide retirement income. In addition, it is far more convenient to rebalance bond funds with the other asset class funds in your portfolio.

When investing in bonds, two factors determine the risk return tradeoff: maturity and credit. As the maturity of a bond lengthens, the interest rate risk associated with the bond increases. When the credit quality of a bond declines, its default risk increases.

What About Using Bonds For Income?

Investors often use bonds to provide income in retirement. While bonds pay steady income, using bonds solely for income can present some risks.

Investing in bonds to provide sufficient cash flow for retirement often means purchasing some bonds with longer maturities and lower credit quality. Purchasing bonds with longer maturities and lower credit quality increases the yield of the bonds but it also increases risk. A long-term bond can be a poor way to hedge inflation because when inflation rises, the purchasing power of the bond decreases.

Bonds play an important role in a diversified portfolio. Rather than taking income only from bonds, however, we suggest investing in short-term, high-credit quality bond funds along with stock and real estate funds. Income is distributed pro-rata from all asset classes within the portfolio. This allows you to benefit from the performance of all asset classes and keep your portfolio in balance.

Using Dividends For Income

Some people promote investing mainly in individual stocks that pay dividends for generating income. There are several problems with this approach. First, there is more risk in owning stocks than owning a combination of stocks and bonds. Second, there is more risk in owning a small number of individual stocks than owning hundreds or thousands of stocks in a mutual fund or exchange traded fund. Third, by owning mainly dividend paying stocks, you lack diversification among other asset classes. All asset classes go through up and down cycles, including large company value stocks, which are typically higher dividend paying stocks. Modern Portfolio Theory and other academic research have shown that combining multiple asset classes in a portfolio and using a total return approach with systematic distributions from multiple asset classes is a most prudent strategy for minimizing risk while enhancing return. For more information on portfolio distribution strategies, see chapter ten.

Rebalancing Your Investments

An effectively diversified portfolio is constructed using many asset classes. Because asset classes do not always move in unison, the amount of money you have in each asset class will change as markets fluctuate.

Although the asset allocation decision is one of the most important elements of you achieving your investment objective, it only works if the allocation is adhered to over time and through varying market environments. Periodic rebalancing is necessary to bring the portfolio back in line with your target allocation. A 2010 research paper conducted by Vanguard [21] concluded that for most broadly diversified portfolios, the asset allocation should be checked annually or semiannually, and the portfolio should be rebalanced if it has deviated more than five percentage points from the target.

Rebalancing is a simple concept, but realizing the benefits of it is a challenge for most investors because it often involves selling investments that have recently done well and buying investments that have recently done poorly. It is emotionally difficult to sell top-performing investments and sell under-performing investments. Over long periods of time, however, asset class performance tends to be mean- reversionary. This means that periods of above-average returns are often followed by periods of below-average returns and eventually revert back to a historical average return. Rebalancing helps you to take advantage of these cycles by systematically selling high and buying low and, most importantly, it keeps you at your chosen level of risk.

Fund Of Funds

Fund of funds have become increasingly popular in recent years and are offered in both mutual funds and hedge funds. These funds are also known as all-in-one funds or multi-management funds. A mutual fund of funds is a type of mutual fund that invests in other mutual funds instead of directly investing in stocks or bonds. They offer a simple way for investors to invest in a broad mix of asset classes as opposed to buying multiple individual mutual funds each representing a distinct asset class.

An advantage of a fund of funds is they allow investors without a lot of money the ability to achieve widespread diversification, perhaps including stocks, bonds, real estate and other asset classes in a single investment. The biggest disadvantage of investing in a mutual fund of funds is the added layer of cost. The expense ratio of the fund of funds is typically considerably higher than investing in the individual funds owned inside the fund of funds.

While I like the concept of fund of funds, I think families selling a farm or ranch will be better served by working with an advisor that uses the low-cost investment solutions suggested in this book and who charges reasonable fees.

Investing On Your Own In The Stock And Bond Market

In my experience, farmers and ranchers are very independent and self-reliant. They like to do things by themselves rather than hire someone to do it for them. This do-it-yourself mindset can hurt them when it comes to financial planning and investing. Although it is not that difficult to invest in the stock and bond market on your own today, a good investment advisor should be able to help you achieve as good or better investment performance than you can achieve on your own net of their fees. They will also provide value through the ongoing advice they offer.

Many investors who manage their own money tend to earn inferior returns over time compared to what the market returns. To prove this, I refer you to a study by a leading investment research firm called DALBAR, Inc.

Since 1994, DALBAR, Inc. has conducted their Quantitative Analysis of Investor Behavior (QAIB) study. This study compares investors' returns against market returns. The results have consistently shown that the average investor earns less – in many cases, much less than the overall market indices. [22] Based on the results of this study, it is no wonder why many have a negative view of the stock market.

The Average Investor vs. The Market				
QAIB 2015 with returns as of December 31, 2014				
	Investor Returns		Index Returns	
	Equity Funds	Bond Funds	S&P 500	Barclay's Aggregate Bond Index
30 year	3.79%	0.72%	11.06%	7.36%
20 year	5.19%	0.80%	9.85%	6.20%
10 year	5.26%	0.69%	7.67%	4.71%

Returns are for the period ending December 31, 2014. Average equity investor and average bond investor performance results are calculated using data supplied by the Investment Company Institute. Investor returns are represented by the change in total mutual fund assets after excluding sales, redemptions and exchanges. This method of calculation captures realized and unrealized capital gains, dividends, interest, trading costs, sales charges, fees, expenses and any other costs. After calculating investor returns in dollar terms, two percentages are calculated for the period examined: Total investor return rate and annualized investor return rate. Total return rate is determined by calculating the investor return dollars as a percentage of the net of the sales, redemptions and exchanges for each period.

Emotions And Investing

Investing can provoke strong emotions. One of the main reasons investors underperform the market is they make decisions based on emotion or "gut feelings". More often than not, these emotional investment decisions do not end up well. Benjamin Graham, often referred to as "the father of investing," said it best; "the investor's chief problem – even his worst enemy – is likely to be himself."

The Cycle Of Market Emotions

This chart represents market cycles and the emotions investors often experience. Investors who make investment decisions based on emotion tend to buy high and sell low. A good investment advisor will help you develop an investment plan that is suitable for you and prevents you from making costly emotional decisions.

Should I Invest In An Annuity?

Annuities are investment vehicles that, in my opinion, are oversold by many individuals. This is largely due to the lucrative commissions the insurance companies pay to those that sell them and because they are heavily promoted by the insurance companies who create them. Annuities may seem like a wise investment, especially in times of high market volatility, but they often have significant drawbacks that aren't often readily apparent or disclosed. Annuities can be very complex with many moving parts, confusing restrictions for obtaining benefits and they can be expensive to own.

While annuities can play a part in an overall diversified investment portfolio, I am of the opinion (and so are most independent, fee-only registered investment advisors) that an investor is better off creating a portfolio of low-cost mutual funds or exchanged traded funds. With that said, here is an overview of annuities.

Annuities are investments offered through insurance companies that can be used to accumulate money on a tax-deferred basis and to provide a contractually guaranteed income for retirement or other purposes. All guarantees of annuities are based upon the financial stability of the insurance company issuing the annuity policy.

There are two basic types of annuities: immediate annuities and deferred annuities. Immediate annuities are purchased solely for generating income. When you purchase an immediate annuity, you select a period of time you would like to receive income. This can be a number of years or for your lifetime. The immediate annuity then pays you a guaranteed amount of income for the period you select.

Deferred annuities are designed to accumulate money for retirement on a tax-deferred basis. Deferred annuities come in three types:

1. Fixed
2. Indexed
3. Variable

Each type has two main phases, the savings phase in which you invest money into the account, and the income phase, in which the plan is either annuitized (converted into a guaranteed stream of income like an immediate annuity) or withdrawals are taken as periodic distributions.

Fixed Annuity

A fixed annuity is similar to a certificate of deposit in that the insurance company pays a guaranteed interest rate for a specified period of time. After that initial specified time is up, the insurance company pays a rate of interest based upon the interest rate environment at the time. When purchasing a fixed annuity, make sure to research the history of the insurance company's renewal rates, as well as the company's financial stability. Most fixed annuities have a minimum guaranteed interest rate that the insurance company will pay regardless of economic conditions, typically about 3%. While fixed annuities generally do not suffer losses due to their guarantees, other less restrictive investments may provide similar returns.

Equity-Indexed Annuity

An equity-indexed annuity (EIA) is a type of fixed annuity that earns interest linked to the performance of a stock or bond index. One of the most commonly used indices is the Standard & Poor's 500 Composite Stock Price Index (the S&P 500). An equity-indexed annuity is different from other fixed annuities because of the way it credits interest to your annuity's value. Most fixed annuities only credit interest calculated at a rate set in the contract. Equity-indexed annuities credit interest using a formula based on changes in the index to which the annuity is linked. The formula decides how the additional interest, if any, is calculated and credited. The sales pitch for EIAs sounds compelling – get upside potential of the stock market with no downside risk. People selling equity index annuities like to talk about the benefits of EIAs and have persuasive presentations on how they are the best thing since sliced bread. What you do not usually hear about are the downsides of an EIA, such as how dividends are excluded from the returns your annuity earns. This is important because historically, dividends have been a strong component of equity returns. Since 1930, dividends have made up approximately 40% of the S&P 500's average annual total return. [23] Other information that is typically not disclosed by the person selling EIAs includes how insurance companies have the flexibility to change features and fees of the annuity, such as lowering the participation rate, increasing the spreads, or lowering the cap, which lowers your potential returns.

EIAs are very complex and difficult to understand. One of the most comprehensive papers on the problems and complexities of EIAs, was prepared by Craig J. McCann, Ph.D., CFA of the Securities Litigation & Consulting Group, Inc. Forbes featured an article by McCann titled, "The Truth About Equity Index Annuities." In the article, he concluded: "Existing equity-indexed annuities are too complex for the industry's sales force and its target investors to understand the investment. This complexity is designed into what is actually a quite simple investment product to allow the true cost of the product to be completely hidden."

"The high hidden costs in equity-indexed annuities are sufficient to pay extraordinary commissions to a sales force that is not disciplined by sales practice abuse deterrents found in the market for regulated securities." He went on to say, "Unsophisticated investors will continue to be victimized by issuers of equity-indexed annuities until truthful disclosure and the absence of sales practice abuses is assured."

Variable annuities have an explicitly disclosed expense ratio that is subtracted from the account balance on an ongoing basis. With fixed or equity-indexed annuities, however, investors only see their contributions into the account, and a return on the account. This leads many to believe (and many insurance agents to claim) that these annuities are "free" or have no cost (and that any commissions paid to the agent are "paid by the insurance company, not the client").

The reality, however, is that fixed annuities do have ongoing costs. Instead of requiring policy owners to pay the annuity fees and agent's compensation directly out of the account value each year, the costs are subtracted from the annuity company's gross returns in the form of an interest rate spread before paying the net remaining return to the investor. In the case of the indexed annuity, the interest rate spread is subtracted before the remaining yield is invested into options to provide the investor's participation rate in the index being tracked.

In my opinion, if you want the opportunity to capture the gains of the stock market, invest in low-cost, tax-efficient index funds in accordance with your tolerance for risk. If your risk tolerance is low, your portfolio should be comprised mainly of short-term, high credit quality bond funds.

Variable Annuity

A variable annuity combines the characteristics of a fixed annuity with the benefits of owning mutual funds. Often referred to as "mutual funds with an insurance wrapper", variable annuities offer a range of investment options called sub-accounts. The value of your investment as a variable annuity owner will vary depending on the performance of the investment sub-accounts you choose.

Some variable annuities today offer optional "income riders" that promise to "guarantee" withdrawals or minimum returns. These riders offer protection from stock market declines. The cost for purchasing these optional riders, however, can be quite expensive.

One of the biggest reasons for not buying a variable annuity is the high cost associated with owning them. The annual fees for owning a variable annuity with an income rider can easily exceed three percent. For comparison purposes, mutual funds and exchange-traded funds can be purchased for less than one half of one percent.

Taxation Of Annuities

While annuities are in the accumulation phase, no taxes are due on the earnings. So, all dividends, interest and capital gains are automatically reinvested without incurring local, state or federal taxes. However, once withdrawn, all earnings are taxed as ordinary income.

Ordinary income tax rates are currently higher than capital gain rates. Depending on your income, you may pay significantly more taxes with an annuity than you would a mutual fund. Net gains from the sale of mutual fund shares held for more than one year are subject to lower capital gains rates.

Another disadvantage of owning annuities is that beneficiaries of an annuity do not receive a stepped-up basis upon death. Your heirs are required to pay ordinary income tax on the gains in an annuity they inherit. Conversely, money held in stocks or in a stock mutual fund receives a stepped up basis upon death. So by moving assets into variable annuities, some investors have unknowingly hurt their beneficiaries — instead of inheriting assets with a step-up in basis, the beneficiaries receive an inheritance on which income tax needs to be paid on any earnings.

IRC Section 1035 Exchange

IRC section 1035 exchange refers to a provision in the tax code that allows for the direct transfer of accumulated funds in a life insurance policy or annuity policy to another life insurance policy or annuity policy, without creating a taxable event. By utilizing IRC section 1035 exchange, you are able to exchange from one annuity into another annuity without having to pay taxes on the gain in the contract.

Some of the newer annuities have features and benefits that older annuities did not have and it can sometime be an advantage to be able to exchange into the newer annuities. However, some older annuities have more attractive benefits than annuities offered today, such as higher guaranteed interest rates. If you are considering a 1035 exchange, make sure you do your research and that you understand the pros and cons of doing so and document the reasons given for doing an exchange by the agent selling the policy. Exchanging into a new annuity will likely result in a new surrender charge period.

Annuity Surrender Charges And Early Withdrawal Penalties

Most annuities have surrender charges. Surrender charges are costs assessed by insurance companies to an annuity owner if they cash out of the annuity or if they withdraw more than ten percent of the annuity value prior to a specified number of years in the annuity contract, typically five to ten years. A typical surrender charge starts at 7% in the first year of the contract and declines by one percent per year thereafter until it reaches zero. Some annuities have much higher surrender charges.

Similar to an IRA, the IRS imposes a 10% penalty on withdrawals made from an annuity prior to age 59 1/2.

What About Alternative Investments?

Alternative investments include such investments as hedge funds, private equity funds and commodities. A common reason given for owning these types of investments is they provide the opportunity to improve a stock and bond portfolio's diversification while reducing volatility. Proponents claim alternative investments are good diversifiers because they have low correlation with traditional stock and bond investments. Just because an investment may have low correlation with the stock market, however, doesn't justify you owning it.

Alternative investments typically have much higher fees than mutual funds and ETFs. They tend to be riskier investments as well, often using large amounts of leverage (borrowed money), making concentrated bets on asset classes or sectors, and trading excessively. And, while alternative investments are subject to less regulation, they also have less opportunity to publish verifiable performance data.

There is little evidence that alternatives have higher returns than traditional asset classes such as stocks and bonds. My belief is that you do not need to invest in alternative investments. Given their high costs, lack of diversification and insufficient liquidity, you are better off sticking to a properly diversified portfolio of low-cost mutual funds or exchange-traded funds. With that said, let's explore some alternative investments.

Hedge Funds

Hedge funds are private investment funds that engage in a wide range of aggressive strategies that are unavailable to mutual funds. Some of the investment strategies include selling short, leverage, program trading, swaps, arbitrage, and derivatives. The main objective of many of these funds is to deliver stock market returns or better with less volatility.

Some hedge funds are "event driven," meaning they try to gain an edge on the markets based on major events such as wars, oil shortages, economic events, and so on. Some are long/short funds, meaning they bet on some stocks going up and others going down. Some hedge funds buy large stakes in companies and then use those positions to influence management to make dramatic changes to the businesses.

Hedge funds are touted as exclusive investment vehicles that deliver superior performance and reduced volatility compared to the market. However, according to industry research, hedge funds are not outperforming the market and many are going out of business.

According to industry research group Hedge Fund Research, some 416 hedge funds closed over the first half of 2014. In 2013, over one thousand hedge funds shut their doors. Another hedge fund survey, which screened over 900 hedge funds managing assets from $100 million to $1 billion revealed that just one of the top five hedge funds profiled outperformed the S&P 500 total return index over a one-year period with similar results for the past three-and five year returns. And, these were some of the best funds! The S&P 500 total return index in fact outperformed almost every hedge fund in the three years through June 2014. [24]

Let's evaluate hedge funds by looking at five important factors affecting investments: Taxes, fees, risk, transparency and liquidity.

Taxes: Investments that generate high taxes result in lower net returns for the investor. Hedge funds involve frequent trading which results in higher taxes.

Fees: Fees are a major predictor of investment performance. Most hedge funds have very high fees, with the typical fee being an annual management fee of 1.5 to 2 percent whether the portfolio is up or down, plus 20 percent of the profits (if there are profits).

Risk: Hedge fund managers have an incentive to take large risks with your money. If hedge fund manager's get paid a fee no matter what the performance of a fund is plus a huge percentage of the profits, they are highly incentivized to take large risks with your money. And, because hedge funds are exempt from many of the rules and regulations governing other mutual funds, they are allowed to take risks that mutual fund manager's cannot take.

Lack of Transparency: Associated with the higher risk of hedge funds is the fact that hedge funds do not regularly disclose what they own or what their investment strategy is.

Liquidity: Hedge funds lack liquidity. Hedge fund investors usually need to wait for "windows" to open so they can redeem their funds. They typically limit opportunities to redeem shares to four times a year or less, and often impose a "lock-up" period of one year or more, during which you cannot cash in your shares.

Warren Buffett's Million-Dollar Hedge Fund Bet

Warren Buffet has repeatedly said that it is very difficult to beat the market and that most investors should invest in index funds. In 2008, Warren Buffet made a 10-year bet with Ted Seides, a partner at the hedge fund company, Protégé. Under the terms of the wager, Buffett is betting (with his own money, not Berkshire's) on the stock market performance of an S&P 500 index fund while Protégé Partners, a New York money manager, is banking on a hedge fund of funds carefully selected by Protégé at the outset. The loser of the bet will donate $1 million to the other's favorite charity.

At the end of 2015, Buffett's position in the S&P 500 Index Fund had posted a return of 65.67%, while the selection of hedge funds was up 21.87%. [25]

In summary, if you want to pay more taxes on your investments, incur much higher fees, potentially expose yourself to excessive risk, not be able to see what you own, lose the ability to exit the investment whenever you wish and potentially increase the odds of underperforming the market, hedge funds are the right investment for you. My recommendation is to stay away from hedge funds and stick to a globally diversified portfolio of low cost index or asset class mutual funds.

Private Equity

Private equity is a general classification that includes the investment in start-up companies, venture capital, and financing throughout phases of a company's growth. Private equity is an ownership interest in a company or portion of a company that is not publicly owned or traded on a stock exchange.

Venture Capital is a subset of private equity specializing in the investment in early-stage to growth-stage companies. Firms will specialize in early stage investing, raising funds from high net worth and institutional capital and deploying them to companies ranging in industry, geography, and funding stages. Venture Capital is an important source of funding for startups that do not have access to capital markets.

There are private equity and venture capital funds one can invest in which provide direct exposure to private companies. These funds have high fees and gaining access to the top-performing private funds is almost impossible for small investors. Private equity investments are also illiquid.

It can take many years for a private equity firm to invest your money and years more to realize positive returns. Most private equity funds limit the ability of an investor to access their funds. Similar to hedge funds, private equity fund fees are typically around two percent and twenty percent of profits. Venture capital funds have similar compensation arrangements and liquidity restrictions.

The Kauffman Foundation, based in Kansas City, Missouri, is among the largest private foundations in the United States with an asset base of approximately $2 billion. In May of 2012 they released a report titled: "We Have Met The Enemy… And He Is Us." In their report, they revealed their experience of investing more than $500 million in nearly 100 venture capital funds over nearly 25 years. Their findings revealed that the majority of venture capital funds underperformed the publicly available small cap stock index.

The report went on to say: "Over the past decade, public stock markets have outperformed the average venture capital fund and for 15 years, VC funds have failed to return to investors the significant amounts of cash invested, despite high-profile successes, including Google, Groupon and LinkedIn." [26]

Not only have the venture capital funds underperformed the market, they did so by taking greater risks, with higher fees and less liquidity. Their report concluded that investors are better off investing in a small cap index fund than a venture capital fund.

In summary, private equity investments have higher fees, are less diversified, more leveraged and less liquid than mutual funds and exchange-traded funds.

Commodities

Agricultural families are familiar with commodities and often like to invest in them. Along with grain, livestock and other agricultural products, commodities include natural resources such as gold, silver, oil and gas. Besides directly owning commodities, a person can invest in commodities through mutual funds, exchange traded funds or futures contracts.

Proponents of commodities claim they are good diversifiers because they have low correlation with stocks and bonds and are a good hedge against inflation. While the price of commodities, such as oil and gold, tend to rise during periods of inflation, commodity prices tend to fall harder during periods of deflation. An example of this was seen in 2008 during the Great Recession. The price of crude oil started in July 2008 around $140 a barrel and just four months later, the price plummeted to $40.

Unlike stocks, bonds and real estate, commodities do not pay any interest or dividends. The only thing commodity funds have going for them is the hope that someone will pay a higher price in the future. Of course, if your timing is wrong, you're going to join the millions of investors who have suffered severe losses speculating in this asset class.

Many of the most reputable investment advisors I know do not include any commodities in their portfolios. I think it is okay to include a commodity fund in your portfolio as long as it doesn't exceed 5% or so of your holdings. One thing to keep in mind is that a diversified stock fund will provide significant commodity exposure through ownership of companies involved in agriculture, mining, oil and gas and other natural resources.

Should I Invest In Gold?

> **Gold gets dug out of the ground in Africa, or someplace. Then we melt it down, dig another hole, bury it again, and pay people to stand around guarding it. It has no utility. Anyone watching from Mars would be scratching his head.**
>
> – Warren Buffett

When the economy and financial markets are struggling, you're likely to hear a lot of advertisements promoting gold as a great investment. When you examine the facts, however, gold is a lousy investment.

Proponents of gold claim that most investor's portfolios should have a significant allocation to gold. They claim the benefits of owning gold include a strong, long-term return, a hedge against inflation, and safe haven during turbulent times. Let's look at historical returns of gold to help you evaluate whether you should invest in gold.

Historically, gold has performed worse than stocks, real estate, energy and bonds and has barely kept pace with inflation. There have been times when gold has performed very well. During the 1970's and from 2000 through 2011, gold outperformed most other asset classes. From 1980 – 1999, gold experienced a negative return after inflation of -6.5%, vs. strong positive returns for stocks. From 1970 through 2005, consumer prices more than doubled while gold lost 20% of its value. From 1971 – 2014, gold performed worse than U.S. and non-U.S. stocks on an inflation-adjusted basis. If you go all the way back to 1802, gold really looks bad. If you bought one dollar of gold in 1802, it would have been worth about $3.21 in 2013. If you had invested one dollar in bonds in 1802, it would have been worth $1,505 and if you invested one dollar in the U.S. stock market, you would have earned $930,550. [27]

Stocks are productive assets that generate growing levels of income and dividends over time. Gold, on the other hand, produces no income and even costs money to own. In contrast, a stock reflects ownership in a business enterprise that seeks to generate profits and produce wealth.

If you own gold, you can expect to not receive an income, pay higher taxes on your returns, experience more volatility than stocks and earn a long-term return lower than bonds. That doesn't sound like a good investment to me.

Working With Local Advisors

In my experience, agricultural families are very loyal people and prefer to do business with people in their community. While I respect the idea of supporting advisors in your community, I caution you on hiring someone to plan for the sale of your farm or ranch and to invest your sale proceeds based largely on you knowing and liking the person.

I have worked with some excellent advisors in small towns. I have also witnessed people receive lousy tax and investment advice because their local advisors did not have extensive experience in advanced tax planning strategies or investing. Just as you would likely get a second opinion from an out of town doctor if you needed heart surgery, I recommend you get second opinions on planning for the sale of your property and managing the money you've spent a lifetime to accumulate.

Selecting The Right Advisor

Choosing the right person to manage your money is critical. You and your family's financial security depends on the guidance your advisor(s) provide, so choose wisely. Unfortunately, many "advisors" today are concerned more about their own interests than those of their clients and they will do you more harm than good. Even if you are working with an ethical advisor, the company they work for can misguide them. Investment and insurance companies often persuade their representatives to sell products that have high fees because it generates the most revenue for them.

The majority of financial advisors today face conflicts of interest. They get paid more if they sell you certain products, they do not have a fiduciary duty to put your interests first and they work for a company that sells their own proprietary investments. If any of these apply to your situation, you should find another advisor.

Independent Advisor vs. Broker

Most "financial advisors" are considered "Broker-Dealers". A "broker" is defined as any person engaged in the business of facilitating transactions in securities for the account of others. Brokers are paid commissions tied to investments they select for their clients. Brokers operate under the suitability standard. This means the broker must believe their recommendations are suitable for their clients.

Because a broker dealer is not required to meet fiduciary standards, they can recommend investments that pay them a bigger commission, even if there is a product that might actually be better for your situation.

A smaller percentage of financial advisory firms are classified as registered investment advisors. A registered investment advisor (RIA) is someone who has completed the qualifications to be registered with the SEC and with applicable state agencies. Often, a RIA works with high net worth clients to help them manage their assets. A RIA often charges advisory fees based on the percentage of assets that are under management.

Registered investment advisors follow a higher standard called the fiduciary standard. This means they have a fiduciary duty to their clients. As a fiduciary, they are required by law to always act in the client's best interests. RIAs must disclose any conflicts of interest and are prohibited from placing trades that will result in more revenue for them or their firm.

Some advisors can be dually licensed. This means they are both an RIA and a broker. Dually registered advisors are able to sell commissioned based products and therefore face conflicts of interest.

You should work with an independent, fee-only registered investment advisor because they are required to put your interest first and they do not sell commissioned based products. An easy way to determine if an advisor is an independent advisor or a broker is by looking at their website. If it says on their website (usually at the bottom) that "securities are offered by XYZ broker dealer....", the advisor is a broker.

Brokers or dually registered advisors often work with firms that have proprietary funds. Proprietary funds are funds owned by the company. Companies typically profit more from their proprietary funds so they are more likely to push those funds.

Custody

> **Brokerages and advisers should have independent custodians and the government should have forced me to have an independent custodian. Client funds should be held by independent custodians. If they had, I would have been caught long ago. If I had had an inspection by the SEC, they would have looked at the custodian accounts and seen the funds on my books did not match the funds in the accounts, and I would have been caught.**
>
> – Bernie Madoff

Financial fraud is a big problem today. One of the best ways to protect your money is to require that your investment account be held with an independent third-party custodian.

Custodians are financial institutions that hold customers' securities for safekeeping so as to minimize the risk of their theft or loss. A custodian holds securities and other assets in electronic or physical form. Since they are responsible for the safety of assets and securities that may be worth hundreds of millions or even billions of dollars, custodians generally tend to be large and reputable firms. Examples of custodians are TD Ameritrade, Fidelity and Charles Schwab.

By placing your investments with an independent third-party custodian, you are creating a layer of safety between your money and your advisor. The custodian serves as the gatekeeper and watchdog for your account.

Advisors who place their client's money with an independent custodian only have access to their clients' accounts to manage their portfolio and place trades on their behalf. They cannot withdraw or transfer funds to an outside account (unless that account is in the client's name and they authorize such a transfer in writing).

If an independent custodian suspects fraudulent activity of any kind, they contact the account holder or report the advisor to the appropriate regulators.

Custodians also send out quarterly statements directly to each client that details all activity in their account, including deposits, withdrawals, trades, and any management fees that were deducted. This provides the investor with full transparency regarding their money and an official record of their account.

Although nothing can provide 100% protection from fraud, working with an independent custodian and a registered investment advisor (RIA) that puts your interests first as a fiduciary will greatly reduce your risk.

Competence

Effective planning for the sale of a farm or ranch requires knowledge of complex financial tools and strategies. In addition to selecting someone who is an independent, fee-only registered investment advisor, it is very beneficial to work with someone who understands the unique challenges and opportunities of agricultural families and is experienced in using the 1031 exchange and charitable remainder trust.

Unbiased Advice

Your advisor should give unbiased advice. One thing I've noticed over the years is that many investment advisors will not suggest using a 1031 exchange because they do not have a real estate license and cannot profit from selling real estate. Most investment advisors want you to pay taxes on the sale of your property so you have cash to invest with them. Likewise, many advisors will not recommend a charitable remainder trust because they do not know enough about them. Similarly, if you talk to a real estate agent, they typically won't suggest you use a charitable remainder trust or invest in the stock and bond market. This is because they can only profit if you invest in real estate. I suggest you talk to an advisor who understands and advocates the use of the 1031 exchange and charitable remainder trust and who doesn't try to steer you down one road based on their self-interests.

Guidelines For Selecting An Advisor

Here are some guidelines you can use in selecting a financial advisor:

1. The advisor is independent. Brokerage firms have inventories of products and quotas to meet, as well as company sponsored incentive programs. Being truly independent helps avoid these conflicts of interest.

2. The advisor is compensated solely by the fees his clients pay him or her. A fee-only advisor is different than a fee-based advisor. Fee-based advisors may still sell commissioned based products. Advisors who are paid commissions on the products they sell and/or on the trades they place face a conflict of interest. They may be influenced to sell products that pay higher commissions or place excessive trades in an account.

3. Uses low-cost investment products. Just because an advisor is a fee-only advisor doesn't mean the fees on the products they sell aren't high. You should work with an advisor who uses low-cost investment products.

4. The advisor uses a passive rather than an active investment management style. As you've seen, the odds of active managers outperforming their passive index benchmark are very small.

5. The advisor uses a consultative process. They take a comprehensive, planned approach to managing your wealth versus just selling you investments.

6. Uses a team approach. A good advisor will collaborate with a team of other professional advisors such as: CPA, attorney, charitable giving specialist, insurance specialist, 1031 exchange intermediary and real estate agent. A collaborative, team approach helps to ensure that every area of your financial

life is properly addressed.

7. The advisor has many years of experience, is trustworthy and is someone you get along well with.

Summary

Obtaining professional advice on how to invest the proceeds from the sale of your farm or ranch is critical. How you invest the sale proceeds will dictate the lifestyle you enjoy during retirement and the inheritance you leave to your children and grandchildren.

The stock and bond market has historically outpaced inflation and provided returns that have significantly outperformed other "safe" investments such as CDs. If you want to earn the returns offered by the stock and bond market, you need to rid yourself of misconceptions you may have about the stock and bond market and learn to avoid the common mistakes investors make.

While there are many strategies for investing in the stock and bond market today, they all boil down to two main philosophies; active vs. passive management. While many advisors promote an active management approach, research shows that a very small percentage of active money managers outperform their passive index benchmark.

Asset allocation is the main factor in determining the performance of a portfolio. The asset classes you choose to invest in and the percentage of your portfolio that you allocate to each asset class will likely have a greater impact on your portfolio's return than anything else.

Academic research has discovered that the size, price and profitability of a company account for almost all of the performance of stocks. By structuring a portfolio with higher weightings to small, value and highly profitable companies, you can seek to receive higher returns over long periods of time.

Creating a globally diversified portfolio of low-cost index funds or asset class funds that is matched to your tolerance for risk is a smart way to invest. Markets are volatile and all asset classes move up and down at random times. Rather than attempting to picks stocks and time the market, it is best to own multiple asset classes through low cost mutual funds or exchange traded funds and adhere to a buy and hold approach.

Many financial advisors face conflicts of interest and are incentivized to sell products that pay high commissions or to trade often to generate fees for themselves. Working with an experienced, independent, fee-only registered investment advisor is one way to improve the chances of obtaining good investment advice.

CHAPTER 9

Investing 1031 Exchange Sale Proceeds

In order to defer taxes on the sale of appreciated land with the IRC section 1031 exchange, an investor must purchase (exchange into) other real estate. Contrary to what many agricultural families think, land does not need to be exchanged for other land. You can exchange land into many types of investment property, such as office buildings, rental houses, apartment complexes, storage facilities, retail strip malls etc. Ironically, a family that is selling land and investing the proceeds into other types of property can often triple their income without having to work nearly as hard for it.

Income Producing Real Estate

The goal for most families who have sold their farm or ranch and are transitioning into retirement is to generate income. Most families want secure income producing real estate they do not have to personally manage.

While land can offer tremendous appreciation potential, it does not offer the cash flow returns you can generally achieve with other types of income producing real estate. For that reason, this chapter will educate you on things you should know, or at least be aware of, when investing in income producing real estate investments besides land.

Commercial vs. Residential Property

One of the first decisions you face when considering the different types of income producing real estate to invest in is deciding whether to invest in commercial or residential real estate.

The term commercial real estate is a broad term. It generally refers to any property other than a single family home or a residential lot in a neighborhood. It is property used solely for business purposes whereas residential real estate is a type of property containing either a single family or multifamily structure used for non-business purposes.

Positive Reasons To Invest In Commercial Property

There are advantages to investing in commercial versus residential real estate. Some of these advantages include:

Higher Income Potential

A big reason for investing in commercial property is higher income potential. Commercial properties generally provide cash flow returns that exceed those offered with rental houses or duplexes.

Triple Net Leases

Another reason for investing in commercial property is that many properties offer triple net leases. This is a type of lease where you, as the property owner, do not have to pay expenses on the property (as would be the case with residential real estate). The lessee (tenant) in a triple net lease is responsible for all property related expenses.

Long Leases

Typically, residential properties have short-term leases. Commercial leases, on the other hand, offer leases for multiple years. Some commercial properties offer leases up to fifteen or twenty years. Longer leases offer cash flow stability.

Interests Of Landlord and Tenant Are Better Aligned

Tenants of commercial properties usually have a vested interest in maintaining the appearance of the building because it affects their business. Keeping the property in good shape may help to increase the investment value for the property owner over time.

Less Property Management Headaches

Commercial property tenants usually go home each night. This means there is less of a chance you will have to deal with maintenance issues in the middle of the night. Business owners also tend to be more professional and easier to work with than residential tenants.

Positive Reasons To Invest In Residential Property

While there are many benefits to owning commercial property, there are benefits to residential properties. Some of these include:

Shorter Vacancy Periods

When a commercial property goes vacant, it can stay vacant for months or even years. Commercial buildings are often designed specifically for a tenant. If that tenant leaves, it could take a long time to re-lease the property and you may incur costs to renovate the building for a new tenant.

Simpler Leases

Residential property leases are less complex than commercial properties.

Simpler Maintenance Issues

Repairs and maintenance issues on residential properties are usually simpler than those of commercial properties. Commercial properties often require licensed professionals. This is not always the case with residential properties.

Smaller Investment

Residential properties typically require a smaller investment than commercial properties. This may allow you to purchase several residential properties and create more diversification with your sale proceeds.

Types Of Commercial Income Producing Property

There are many types of commercial income producing real estate you can invest in. The main types are:

Office Property

Office buildings are a popular investment because they can serve a wide variety of tenants, are often in prime downtown locations and can be offered with a triple or double net lease.

Retail Property

Retail property is a classification of zoning for property that is used for a store, shopping center or service business. There is a wide variety of retail properties, ranging from large shopping malls to small, single tenant buildings. Retail properties can also serve a wide variety of tenants and are offered with triple net leases.

Industrial Property

Warehouses, distribution centers and assembly plants are all examples of industrial real estate. Industrial properties are generally easier to manage and have lower operating expenses than office and retail properties. They also typically require a smaller investment than office or retail properties.

Multi-Family Residential Property

Multi-family properties include apartment complexes or high-rise apartment buildings. Generally, anything larger than a four-plex is considered commercial real estate.

A positive aspect of multi-family is that no matter what the economy is doing, people always need a place to live. Therefore, occupancy levels tend to stay fairly high. Even though you have to deal with many tenants in a multi-family property, there can be lower maintenance costs than a single family home because you only have one front door, one lawn to mow and one roof to repair or replace. A disadvantage of multi-family is one problem renter can create problems for the other tenants and may cause tenants to vacate the property.

Miscellaneous

This catch-all category would include any other properties such as hospitality, medical, self-storage, assisted living, as well as many others.

Mixed Use

Some properties are referred to as "mixed-use" because the property contains a mix of more than one property type. For example, a building may offer retail space on the first floor and office or apartment units on the second and higher floors.

Alternative Types Of Real Estate Investments

Three alternative types of real estate investments that are worth mentioning are REITs, TICs and DSTs.

REITs

A REIT is a corporation that purchases, owns and manages real estate properties and/or real estate loans. You can purchase shares in a REIT much like a mutual fund. While REITs can be a good investment, you cannot do a 1031 exchange into shares of a REIT because the shares of a REIT are considered personal property even though the REIT, at the entity level, owns real property assets.

An UPREIT (Umbrella Partnership Real Estate Investment Trust) is an alternative to a section 1031 like-kind exchange. Instead of selling the property, the owner contributes it to an UPREIT in exchange for securities called "operating partnership units" or "limited partnership units." Unlike selling the property, this transaction doesn't create a taxable event.

UPREITs are complex investments. If you want to defer tax on the sale of appreciated real estate, I suggest you use the 1031 exchange and stick to investing in fee-simple real property that you own and control.

TICs And DSTs

A TIC (Tenant-In-Common) real estate investment is an investment in which two or more parties own a fractional interest in a given property, usually commercial real estate. TICs are eligible for a 1031 exchange and were popular real estate investments prior to the recession of 2008 and 2009. TICs are complex investments that can involve high risks, high costs and liquidity problems. Again, if you are looking for 1031 replacement property, I suggest you stick to fee-simple real estate you own and control yourself.

Another co-owned property investment which is eligible as 1031 exchange replacement property is DSTs (Delaware Statutory Trust). A DST is a separate legal entity created as a trust under the laws of Delaware in which each owner has a "beneficial interest" in the DST for Federal income tax purposes and is treated as owning an undivided fractional interest in the property. While the DST structure effectively deals with some of the problems with TICs, they are also a more complex real estate investment.

Tenant Credit Rating

The value of commercial income producing real estate is largely based on the financial security of the tenant. You want to make sure your tenant can pay their rent and meet all terms of a lease. If the tenant defaults on their lease, you could end up with an empty building and you are stuck with paying all the property expenses. Examining a tenant's credit rating is one way to prevent this situation from happening.

Publically traded companies are assigned letter grades based upon their financial strength. Three of the most reputable credit rating companies are Standard and Poor's (S&P), Moody's, and Fitch.

S&P assigns credit ratings that range from "AAA," which signifies an "extremely strong capacity to meet financial commitments, to "D," which indicates "payment default on financial commitments." Investment grade properties have a rating of "BBB" or higher. A BBB rating indicates that a company has "adequate capacity to meet financial commitments, but is more subject to adverse economic conditions."

Classes Of Property

Office buildings are generally classified into one of four categories: Class A, Class B, Class C or Class D. Each classification represents a different level of risk and return. These letter grades are assigned to properties and areas by factors such as age of the building, tenant income levels and property amenities to name a few.

Class A properties represent the highest quality buildings in their market. They are generally buildings constructed within the last 15 years. They are nice looking properties with little to no deferred maintenance (postponed repairs), the best amenities and the highest income-earning tenants. These properties are usually located in desirable areas and demand the highest rents.

Class B properties are older than Class A properties, typically built within the last 15-20 years. They often have deferred maintenance issues and rent for slightly lower rates than Class A properties. These properties may offer the opportunity for an investor to renovate the property and have it upgraded to Class A.

Class C properties are typically more than 25 years old with much fewer, if any, amenities. These properties are often in need of renovation. Because of this, Class C buildings tend to have lower rental rates in a market with other Class A or B properties.

Class D properties are older buildings in less than desirable neighborhoods and potentially dangerous areas. They are older buildings with no amenities, large amounts of deferred maintenance, functional obsolescence, and the tenants can be difficult to work with. Although these properties can offer good cash flow returns, the cash flow is often greatly reduced due to repairs and lack of payment by tenants.

Classifications are also assigned to areas. Area classes as follows:

A. Newer growth areas
B. Older, stable areas
C. Older, declining, or stable areas
D. Older, declining, potentially rapidly declining areas

Cautions Of Investing Locally

I have known agricultural families who have exchanged their land into properties located in the towns closest to their farm or ranch. While it is nice to have a property close to where you live from a management perspective, properties located in a rural area or a small city may not offer the income potential, appreciation potential and financial security that a similar property located in a strong market might offer. Do not limit your search to areas near your home that may have poor demographics and limited potential for growth. Hiring a property management firm makes it possible to invest in properties outside your immediate geographic area.

Evaluating Income Producing Real Estate Investments

Effectively analyzing income properties can be very complex and is something best left to professionals. A commercial real estate investment professional can help you identify and evaluate income producing real estate investments. With that said, here are some things you should understand when evaluating income producing real estate investments.

Location, Location, Location

We've all heard the statement that the most important thing about investing in real estate is the property's location, location, location. Good locations vary depending on the type of property you are looking for. Ideally, good investment properties should be located in an area with low vacancy rates and a limited availability of space. Low supply and high demand means favorable rental rates, as well as the potential for a higher rate of appreciation.

Demographics

The strength of the local economy of an area will affect the value of your investment so be sure to research the demographics of an area before you invest. Demographics are the study of a population based on factors such as economic status, level of education, income level and employment. Properties located in areas with rising incomes and strong population growth better position you for properties that experience lower vacancies, rising rents and growth of your investment over time. If your property is in a location with poor demographics, your property may lose tenants and decline in value over time.

It Is All About The Numbers

While location, supply and demand and good demographics are important factors in evaluating real estate investments, when it comes to investing in cash flow real estate, one is mainly interested in buying the income stream the property offers. Therefore, the most important factor for evaluating income producing real estate investments are the numbers.

Investors use many different approaches to evaluate investment properties. You should be familiar with the different approaches as you begin your property search. Before discussing some of these approaches, it will be helpful to understand a couple of terms.

Net Operating Income

Net Operating Income or NOI is simply the annual income generated by an income-producing property after taking into account all income collected from operations and deducting all expenses incurred from operations. NOI helps income producing real estate investors evaluate investment properties.

Operating expenses are those costs required to run and maintain a building and the ground it is located on. Operating expenses include items such as insurance, property taxes, advertising, property management fees, landscaping, snow removal, utilities, repairs and janitorial fees. NOI is a before-tax figure; it also excludes principal and interest payments on loans, capital expenditures, depreciation and amortization.

Ratios And Quotients Used To Evaluate Income Producing Real Estate Investments

Below, are five ratios and quotients commonly used to evaluate income-producing real estate investments.

1. Capitalization Rate

The Capitalization Rate or Cap Rate is a ratio used to estimate the value of income producing properties. It equals the net operating income divided by the sales price or value of a property expressed as a percentage.

Cap rates are one of many financial tools used by investors to establish a purchase price for an investment property in a given real estate market.

Cap rates based on figures from recent transactions of buyers and sellers provide the best market value estimates for a property. If you are able to obtain reliable cap rate data, you can then use this information to estimate what similar income properties should sell for. This will help you to determine whether or not the asking price for a particular piece of property is too high.

$$\text{Cap Rate} = \frac{\text{NOI}}{\text{Value}} \qquad \text{Estimated Property Value} = \frac{\text{NOI}}{\text{Cap Rate}}$$

Example 1
A property has a NOI of $140,000 and the asking price is $2,000,000.
The Cap Rate = $140,000 / $2,000,000 = 7.00%

Example 2
An office building has a NOI of $150,000 and Cap Rates in the area for this type of property are 8%.
Estimated Property Value = $150,000 / 8% = $1,875,000

2. Net Income Multiplier

The Net Income Multiplier or NIM is a factor used to estimate the market value of income producing real estate. It is calculated by dividing the market value of a property by the net operating income of the property.

$$NIM = \frac{Market\ Value}{Net\ Operating\ Income}$$

Example 1 — An apartment complex has a NOI of $150,000 and a market value of $1,200,000. The NIM is $1,200,000 / $150,000 = 8

Example 2 — The average net income multiplier for similar properties in a particular area is 8 and the net operating income for a similar property is $100,000.
The market value is 8 X $100,000 = $800,000

$$Market\ Value = NIM \times NOI$$

The net income multiplier and the cap rate are financial tools used to estimate the market value of income properties. The cap rate is better known and more widely used. The cap rate and the NIM produce identical results when estimating the market value of an income property since the net income multiplier is the inverse of the cap rate. The cap rate is equal to 100 divided by the NIM and conversely the NIM is equal to 100 divided by the cap rate.

$$Cap\ Rate = \frac{100}{NIM} \qquad NIM = \frac{100}{Cap\ Rate}$$

3. Cash On Cash Return

Cash on Cash Return (CCR) is helpful in evaluating the profitability of income producing properties. CCR is a percentage that measures the return on cash invested in an income producing property.

Cash on Cash Return is calculated by dividing the before-tax cash flow of a property by the amount of cash invested in the property and is expressed as a percentage. For example, if the cash flow for an investment property before taxes is equal to $100,000 and the amount of cash invested in the property is $1,200,000, the cash on cash return is equal to 8.33%.

$$CCR = \frac{\text{Before-tax Cash Flow}}{\text{Cash Invested}}$$

4. Gross Rent Multiplier

The Gross Rent Multiplier (GRM) is a ratio used to estimate the value of income producing properties. When comparing similar properties in the same area or location, the lower the GRM, the more profitable the property from an income perspective. If current information is available, the average GRM of similar properties sold in an area can be used to estimate the value of other properties of the same type. The GRM is calculated by dividing the sales price by the monthly or annual potential gross income.

The GRM can provide a rough estimate of a property's value when consistent and accurate financial information is available. However, a property's operating expenses, debt service and tax consequences are not included in the GRM calculation. You could have two properties with the same potential gross income but vastly different operating expenses. In such a case, the above formula may result in inaccurate estimations of these property's values. The GRM formula also doesn't account for vacancies which could impact the accuracy of the property value estimates. This is why it is very important to have accurate and detailed financial information on comparable sales when establishing a GRM or Cap Rate. The capitalization rate is a more reliable tool for estimating the value of income producing properties since vacancy amount and operating expenses are included in the cap rate calculation. The GRM is useful in providing a rough estimate of value.

$$\text{GRM (monthly)} = \frac{\text{Sales Price}}{\text{Monthly Potential Gross Income}}$$

Example 1 — If the sales price for a property is $1,000,000 and the monthly potential gross rental income for the property is $13,333 the GRM is equal to 75.

Example 2 — You have multiple properties that are similar to each other and have recently sold. The average monthly GRM for the properties is 75. Equipped with this information, you can estimate the value of comparable properties for sale. If the monthly potential gross income for a property is $10,000, you would estimate its value in the following way.
Estimated Market Value = GRM x Potential Gross Income= 75 X $10,000 = $750,000

5. Price Per Square Foot

Price per square foot is a method for comparing the values of similar income producing properties in a given location. To calculate the price per square foot of a property, divide the sales price by the total number of square feet of the property. Next, review other similar income properties currently listed for sale in the area to see how much a similarly sized property is priced.

When reviewing properties in an area, ask your real estate agent to pull a list of similar properties with comparable values that have sold within the last year in that area. Calculating what properties of similar sizes and with similar amenities have sold for per square foot can help you determine the value of the property.

Keep in mind that the price per square foot of properties can vary widely based on a number of factors such as the amenities of the property, the quality of construction, location, credit rating of tenant etc.

$$\text{Price Per Square Foot} = \frac{\text{Cost of Property}}{\text{Number of Square Feet}}$$

Due Diligence

Due diligence is a term commonly used when discussing investment property. It essentially means taking precaution and doing your homework on a property before you make a purchase. Due diligence involves tasks such as reviewing documents, performing calculations, shopping insurance and visiting properties. A primary function of due diligence is to verify information a seller has provided you.

Most real estate purchase contracts provide for a due diligence period after the contract is signed. It typically ranges from 30 to 60 days. The due diligence period is important for both the buyer and the seller. During this time, the buyer conducts an in-depth analysis of the condition of the property and the feasibility of purchasing the property while maintaining the right to terminate the contract if their research turns up anything they do not like.

Areas To Consider When Performing Due Diligence

Property Documents: Property sellers have information that buyers need to evaluate an investment. Property records, such as title reports, property studies, maintenance records, operating expense reports, leases, and financial statements should be given to the buyer. The due diligence provision should require the seller to provide this information to a buyer within a certain number of days from contract execution.

Commencement Of Due Diligence Period: The due diligence period should not begin until the purchase and sales contract has been fully executed and the seller has delivered, per the contract terms, all the records to the buyer. Some sellers request that the due diligence period begin once a letter of intent (LOI) is signed. This could be detrimental to the buyer because they may have to spend money to evaluate the property before the protections offered in a sales contract are in place. The seller could back out if a contract has not been agreed upon and the buyer would have unnecessarily wasted money. Letters of Intent are usually non-binding.

Termination Clause: The purpose of the due diligence period is to allow the buyer to terminate the sale agreement if they choose to not invest. The provision should state that the buyer can terminate for any reason by sending a termination notice before the end of the due diligence period.

Cost Of Due Diligence Studies: A buyer may spend money conducting due diligence on the property. A provision should be included which states that if the seller backs out of the agreement, the buyer receives reimbursement for these due diligence costs.

Cost To Repair Property: It is wise to have an inspection completed on a property by a qualified property inspector during the due diligence period. Make sure you obtain estimates for any work that needs to be completed prior to making the purchase.

Insurance: Before proceeding too far, make sure you can obtain insurance on the property and find out how much it will cost.

Homeowners Association: If you are looking at residential properties, make sure you review the Home Owners Association (HOA) covenants and other documents. Beware of communities that are in poor financial condition or have significant upcoming expenditures.

Title Insurance And Plat: Review the title abstract and insurance policy to see if there are any issues with the property. Talk to the title insurance company and possibly have an attorney review the documents.

Property Taxes: Find out what the property taxes are as this is one of the largest expenses and can increase each year.

Replacement Reserves

Replacement reserves are funds set aside to provide for future capital improvements such as heating and air conditioning systems, roofs, flooring, appliances, parking lot resurfacing etc. This account is separate from funds used for minor repairs and maintenance, such as replacing light bulbs, which are considered routine operating expenses, not irregular capital expenditures. It is important that you maintain adequate replacement reserves to prevent you from having to borrow money or liquidate other investments should the need for capital improvements arise.

The amount you set aside for replacement reserves depends on several factors, such as the age and type of property. Building inspectors can help you determine what items may need to be replaced and the cost of replacement. Many lenders require replacement reserves to be set aside, usually in escrow, to cover major capital expenditures over the term of the loan. You should keep in mind that property sellers and listing real estate agents may exclude replacement reserves from their property summaries in order to increase the net operating income and thus increase the property's valuation.

Lease Agreements

The lease agreement for a commercial income property outlines and details the obligations and responsibilities of the landlord (lessor) and the tenant (lessee). It explains what the landlord and tenant have agreed upon in regards to length of the lease, how much the monthly rent will be, and who will be responsible for upkeep of the property. It governs what the landlord and tenant can and cannot do and serves as a legal, binding contract that will dictate what happens if legal proceedings arise between the two parties. The lease agreement is a critically important document that should be drafted or reviewed by an experienced real estate attorney.

Types Of Commercial Leases

Commercial space may be rented by the square foot or set as a dollar amount per square foot of space. The tenant may be offered one of two different types of leases:

1. Gross Lease. A gross lease mandates a set amount of rent to be paid each month. The owner agrees to pay taxes, insurance and all maintenance on the building.

2. Net Lease. A net lease requires the tenant to pay a portion or all of the taxes, fees and maintenance costs for the property in addition to rent. There are three primary types of net leases: single (net), double (net-net) and triple (net-net-net).

The rent collected in a net lease is net of expenses. Therefore, the rent charged under a net lease is usually lower than rent charged under a gross lease where the lessor is responsible for expenses.

Triple Net Leases

If you've done any research on income producing real estate, you've probably heard the term triple net property or triple net leases (NNN). A triple net lease is popular with investors because it is structured as a turnkey investment. In a triple net lease, the tenant is responsible for paying the three major categories of expenses associated with commercial real estate ownership which are: property taxes, insurance and maintenance.

Investment-Grade Properties

Triple-net properties are often leased to a single tenant and to large companies. Many of these companies have "investment grade" ratings. As stated earlier, investment grade properties have a rating of "BBB" or higher.

Benefits Of Investment-Grade, Long-Term Net-Leases

Simplicity: Triple-net and double-net leases offer investors the ability to enjoy the benefits of real estate ownership without many of the management headaches associated with income properties. Long-term net-leases are generally simple to manage because most of the property expenses are paid by the tenant. If the property is damaged, the tenant is responsible for repairing the property at their own expense.

Income Stability: Investment-grade, long-term net-leases can provide stability of income for investors. Because lease terms are often long and payments typically backed by national companies with strong balance sheets, they likely offer greater protection during tough economic times than smaller companies who may struggle to make lease payments.

Attractive Financing: Long-term leases backed by investment grade tenants may help investors obtain better financing terms from lenders. This can save the investor a lot of money over the life of the loan.

Drawbacks of Investment-Grade, Long-Term Net Leases

Single-Tenant Dependence: The largest drawback to investment-grade, long-term triple net leased real estate is that if your major tenant defaults on their lease, it can be difficult to find another tenant. If there is debt on the property, it can be stressful to make expense payments yourself while searching for another tenant.

Tenant Improvements: Another risk of leasing to a national credit tenant is the likely cost of having to make improvements or modifications to the property to accommodate the tenant.

Upside Limitations: While long-term leases to investment grade tenants may offer downside protection, especially during tough economic times, they may limit your upside growth potential. Unlike commercial properties that have shorter-term leases, such as multi-family properties that can be increased during a growing market, long-term net-leases are fixed for many years and do not allow this flexibility. Therefore, it is less likely that a long-term net-leased property will experience large upside appreciation when you go to sell the property. Though there are often increases built in to the lease agreement, these rent increases are typically limited to one to two percent per year.

Variations of the Triple Net Lease

Single Tenant Net Lease

Triple net leased properties are generally leased to one single tenant and are thus referred to as STNLs or single tenant net leases. A triple net lease property can, however have two or more tenants, though it would not be considered an STNL investment. An example of this would be a retail strip center where all tenants are wrapped into one triple net lease. The risk of default in this arrangement is spread out over more than one tenant. These properties can appeal to investors seeking to reduce the risk from having only one tenant, though they may involve more complexity than having only one tenant.

Double Net Lease

Another variation of the triple net lease is the double net lease where the net's typically refer to property taxes and insurance. Double net leases, like triple net leases, are usually offered on properties leased to a single tenant. In a double net lease, the landlord assumes some of the financial and maintenance obligations.

Double net leased properties generally offer a slightly higher CAP rate than triple net leased investments, because of the maintenance expenses which the owner is responsible for. Brand new double net properties with long-term warranties offered by the builder on the building's structures can be attractive to investors looking for a higher return.

Tenant Improvements

Tenant improvements (TIs) are changes made to the interior of an investment property by its owner to accommodate the needs of a tenant. This may include items such as floor and wall coverings, partitions, heating and air conditioning, fire protection, and security systems. Determining who is responsible for TI costs is usually negotiated between the owner and the tenant, and is usually contained in the lease agreement.

Tenant Improvement Allowance

A tenant improvement allowance or credit is the amount of money a landlord is willing to spend to customize a property for the specific needs of a tenant. This is typically found in the Leasehold Improvements or Concessions section of a commercial lease.

Before a new lease or renewal is signed, landlords are usually willing to negotiate a tenant improvement allowance to replace items such as paint, carpeting, or possibly replacing windows and/or doors. It is fairly common for the owner of a property to grant an allowance for making improvements to the property.

Rent Escalation

Rent escalation is a lease provision in which the tenant is required to pay increased rent during the term of the lease. The rent is usually adjusted annually by an agreed upon method. The most common way to escalate rent is through a "stepped rent" where the square foot rental rates are increased each year.

The Consumer Price Index (CPI) can also be used to determine the rate of rent escalation. Every month the Bureau of Labor Statistics of the U.S. Department of Commerce publishes the CPI, which indicates changes in the cost of living. By using this index to determine the amount of rent to charge, the landlord can feel assured the rent they are charging is keeping pace with the rate of inflation.

A flat fixed-annual-percentage increase in base rent is a way of escalating rent by increasing it by a fixed percentage each year. The disadvantage of a fixed-percentage increase is if the CPI goes higher than the fixed rate, the fixed rate will not be keeping up with inflation.

Leverage

In my experience, most farmers and ranchers prefer to avoid taking on debt (leveraging a property) when investing proceeds from the sale of their farm or ranch. However, because matching the 1031 exchange proceeds exactly with replacement property purchase price can be difficult and because many investors refuse to pay one penny of tax, taking on some debt with the replacement property is common.

Leverage is the use of borrowed money to increase your profits in an investment. The ability to leverage real estate is one of the greatest wealth building aspects real estate offers.

For example, let's assume you have $1,000,000 to invest and you purchase an office building for $1,000,000. If your property appreciated at a rate of seven percent per year, at the end of the first year, your property would be worth $1,070,000. At the end of year two, it is worth $1,144,900. Now let's assume that you put your $1,000,000 down on a $5,000,000 income property, which also appreciates at seven percent per year. At the end of the first year, it is worth $5,350,000. At the end of the second year, it is worth $5,724,500. By borrowing money to purchase a larger income property, you increased your income by $579,600 in just two years!

Placing "positive leverage" on a property allows for investors to effectively increase positive cash flow by borrowing money at a lower cost than the property pays out. For example, if a property is generating a seven percent cash-on-cash return and you're paying five percent interest on your loan, you're paid seven percent on the equity portion and approximately two percent on the money borrowed, thereby leveraging debt.

Let me be clear, I am not advocating that you take on debt when purchasing replacement property. I am simply pointing out there are potential advantages to doing so. If you want to avoid paying taxes and you have a stable income producing property with positive leverage, taking on some debt may not be a bad thing to do. Make sure, however, you have some reserves in case your tenant moves out and you are required to pay the property expenses until a new tenant is secured.

Depreciation

Depreciation is the loss in value of an asset over time due to wear and tear, physical deterioration and age. One of the tax benefits associated with real estate is the ability to deduct the depreciation of the property on your taxes. The depreciation deductions you write-off on your taxes in any year reduces your taxable income for that year, increasing your profit for that year. Capital improvements such as replacing a roof or heating and air conditioning system are subject to the same depreciation laws.

The cost of reproducing an income property can be recovered over the useful life of a property and is determined by law. Only the building, however, and not the land can be depreciated. Residential income property is depreciated over a 27 ½ year period, whereas commercial property is depreciated over 39 years. Both residential and commercial properties are depreciated using straight-line depreciation, which stipulates that an asset must be depreciated by equal amounts each year over its useful life.

Selecting A Real Estate Broker

Income producing real estate carries many risks and can be difficult to properly evaluate for investment. If you plan to invest in income producing real estate, you should work with a professional real estate broker. Engaging the services of a real estate broker may not cost you money out-of-pocket, because the sales commission is often paid entirely by the property seller. With this in mind, there is really no reason not to work with a good real estate broker.

Who you choose to assist you with your real estate investing is a critically important decision. You want to make sure you select someone that has the knowledge, experience and ability to find and evaluate the best property for your needs. And, if you want to invest in income producing real estate investments other than residential properties, you should work with someone that specializes in commercial real estate versus someone who mainly sells residential or farm and ranch property.

A CCIM (Certified Commercial Investment Member) is a recognized expert in the commercial and investment real estate industry. The CCIM designation signifies a person has completed advanced coursework in financial and market analysis, and demonstrated extensive experience in the commercial real estate industry. The CCIM designation represents expertise in financial, market, and investment analysis, in addition to negotiation.

Here are four things to look for when selecting a commercial real estate broker:

Experience In Commercial Transactions

Find out what percentage of the broker's overall transactions are commercial properties. Look for a broker who specializes in and works exclusively with commercial real estate.

Access To Properties And Property Data

Besides being able to view properties the public is allowed to see, real estate brokers utilize multiple real estate databases to uncover all available properties, including "off the market" properties. Find out if your broker subscribes to commercial real estate databases and commercial real estate marketing platforms.

National Marketing Reach

Do not limit yourself to searching for properties in close proximity to your home. Find a broker that has both local market knowledge and expanded reach through a national commercial property network and other sources.

Specialized Training And Experience In Applicable Property Type

If you are mainly interested in a particular type of commercial property such as office or industrial buildings, look for brokers who specialize in that type of property. A person who specializes in a property type likely has a higher level of expertise in that type of property and may be able to better source and evaluate that property type.

Some real estate brokers focus exclusively on a property niche. For example, our team at Solid Rock Realty Advisors specializes in selling and managing office buildings leased to the U.S. federal government. These properties are one of the most secure income producing real estate investments available. They offer the upside potential of commercial real estate with the credit of a U.S. bond.

The General Services Administration (GSA) is the property manager for the federal government. There are over 9000 properties in the United States where the GSA is the tenant and pays rent to a Lessor. Finding available government properties and effectively analyzing them for investment, however, can be difficult. Many newly constructed federal government buildings are owned by the contractors who built them and are not publicly listed for sale. Locating available federal government buildings largely depends on knowing these contractors.

There are also nuances in the leases of federal government leased buildings. One unique feature of a federal lease is the gross rent in the lease is inflation adjusted every year to protect the investor's real return. Another unique aspect of these leases is the property taxes are "frozen" the year after the office building is constructed for a government agency. Because the property taxes are frozen in a federal lease, an investor in federal government buildings doesn't have to worry about rising property taxes.

Some other unique features of the U.S. federal government office building market are:

- Demand for office space is driven by the social mission of federal agencies rather than by economic goals.
- Property values and demand for space is much less sensitive to the volatility of business cycles.
- Standard firm terms within the leases typically have 5, 10 or 15 years with no lease break clauses in the first 10 plus years, i.e., no early lease termination rights.
- Very high historical lease renewal rates.
- Low property operating costs, capital expenditures and reserve requirements.

Hiring A Property Management Firm

A property management company can handle the responsibilities of managing all aspects of your property, freeing you to enjoy the property's income without having to deal with the day-to-day responsibilities of your property.

A good property management firm will do more than just manage the property for you; they will help safeguard your investment, keep your tenants satisfied and help you maximize the return on your investment. Another benefit of hiring a property management company is that it enables you to invest in properties outside your geographic area. If you manage your own properties, you are pretty much limited to properties within a small radius of your home.

Property managers are typically paid a fee or a percentage of the rent brought in for the property while under management. When shopping for a property manager, make sure to compare the rates charged and find out what services they provide. It is a good idea to speak with several customers of the management company to see how satisfied they are with their services.

Things To Look For When Hiring A Property Management Firm

Accreditation: As in other areas of real estate, a property management firm that is accredited is distinguished as having met higher standards. Some property management designations include: Certified Property Manager (CPM) and Real Property Administrator (RPA).

Insurance: Inquire about a firm's insurance coverage and make sure they have a fidelity bond to protect against the loss of money or property through fraudulent or dishonest acts of employees.

Conflicts of interest: Ask the firm to disclose any companies that it may own or use exclusively, such as landscaping or maintenance firms. Where there is potential conflict, make sure the management firm uses a competitive bidding procedure and is willing to provide evidence of this.

Downsides Of Owning Real Estate

Real estate offers some very attractive investment and tax attributes. However, there are potential issues involved with owning real property you should be aware of. These include:

Lack Of Liquidity: Unlike stocks, bonds or mutual funds, which can easily be sold on any given day the market is open, real estate is much harder to sell. It is possible to find yourself stuck with a property you do not want and cannot sell.

Lack Of Diversification: An agricultural family's net worth is often represented almost entirely by the value of their land. If a family exchanges all of their land to defer 100% of the capital gain tax, they may not own enough properties to be adequately diversified.

Property Management: Real estate is not a passive investment. Someone needs to cut the grass, shovel the snow, pay insurance, make repairs, and manage tenants. Many investors simply do not want to hassle with the Four T's – tenants, toilets, trash and turnover. While you can hire a property manager to manage the property for you, that does reduce your income and you still have to make sure your property manager is doing their job.

Hassle Factor: Buying and selling real estate is not a simple process. It takes time to select the right property and the closing process can be stressful and time-consuming. Likewise, selling a property can take a lot of time and create some stress.

Loss Of Income: If you have a tenant that does not renew their lease or who defaults on their payments, you can suffer a loss of income. You may find yourself in a position of having to pay property expenses out of your own pocket. And, if you have debt on the property, you will have to make loan payments. If you are going to invest in real estate, make sure you have ample cash reserves in case the property's income is not sufficient to cover the ongoing expenses.

Liability: If a tenant suffers an injury on your property, they may sue you. Owning real estate in your name makes you personally liable for everything that happens to or on the property. It is best to own your property in some type of an entity such as an LLC and make sure to purchase liability insurance.

Summary

In order to save taxes on the sale of a farm or ranch with a 1031 exchange, the sale proceeds must be invested in real estate. While many prefer to exchange their farm or ranch into land or rental houses, commercial properties may offer higher income potential, longer leases and double or triple net leases where all or most of the major expenses are paid by the tenant.

Effectively analyzing income properties can be very complex and is something best left to professionals. A commercial real estate investment professional can help you identify and evaluate income producing real estate investments and assist you in selecting a firm to manage your properties.

Several ratios and quotients are used to evaluate income producing real estate investments. Some of the most popular include the Capitalization Rate, Net Income Multiplier, Cash on Cash Return, Gross Rent Multiplier and Price Per Square Foot. Having an understanding of these different ratios and quotients can help you become a better investor.

Make sure to do your due diligence prior to purchasing a property and do not let the tax tail waive the investment dog. In other words, do not exchange into a property just to save taxes. Make sure you take the time to find the most suitable real estate investment for your needs and don't be afraid to look outside your local area for investment possibilities.

CHAPTER 10

Retirement Planning Considerations

A gricultural families retiring today face many financial challenges. Low interest rates, volatile stock markets, increasing life expectancies, rising health care costs, uncertainties about Social Security and fears of higher inflation and tax rates have made planning for retirement a difficult task. In addition, news reports on our economy, national debt and homeland security raise fears about our well-being and future financial security. Many today are scared, confused and unsure of how to invest to generate an income that will last as long as they do and that will keep pace with the rising cost of living.

Increasing Life Expectancies

One of the greatest challenges people face today in retirement is longevity. People are living longer due to advances in medical technology. In 1900, the average man was expected to live to age 46. In 1936, the average life expectancy increased to age 63. Today, a married couple age 65 has a 40% chance that one spouse will live to age 95. [28] Investing for a retirement that could last 20 to 40 years requires careful planning.

Rising Healthcare Costs

The cost of health care has skyrocketed in recent years. As we age, health care becomes a much larger portion of our total annual spending. People typically underestimate how much health care will cost them during their retirement years. According to a 2014 study by the Employee Benefit Research Institute, in 2014 a couple would need $247,000 in savings to cover health care expenses in retirement if they wanted a 90 percent chance of having enough savings in retirement to cover their lifetime health care expenses (not including long-term care).[29] If you are age 65 years or older, do you have $247,000 earmarked specifically for health care expenses?

Long Term Care

Long-term care includes home health care, assisted living facilities and skilled nursing home care. Neglecting to factor the cost of long-term care into your retirement planning could prove to be very harmful to your future lifestyle. According to a recent study, at least 70 percent of people over age 65 will need long-term care services at some point in their lifetime. [30]

In 2014, the median annual cost of home health care in the U.S. was $43,472. The median annual cost of a single occupancy bedroom in an assisted living facility was $42,000. The median annual cost of a semi-private room in a nursing home care facility was $77,380. The median annual cost of a private room in a nursing home care facility was $87,600 [31].

Most long-term care costs are not covered by Medicare. If you do not have long-term care insurance or if your long-term care insurance is inadequate, the cost of care could severely affect your retirement lifestyle.

Social Security

Starting in 2033, Social Security trustees project that the system will be able to pay only 77% of promised benefits. [32] For this reason, a number of reforms have been suggested. While most individuals who will be selling their farm or ranch soon will not be affected by these reforms, these reforms could negatively affect future retirees. Some of these proposed reforms include raising the retirement age, raising payroll taxes and revising benefit formulas.

The age you file for Social Security benefits can dramatically affect the lifetime payments you will receive. Filing for Social Security benefits too soon and failing to coordinate benefits with your spouse are common ways that people fail to maximize the income Social Security may provide.

Inflation

As discussed earlier in the book, inflation is a critical factor in retirement planning. As inflation rises, every dollar you own buys a smaller percentage of a good or service. When inflation goes up, there is a decline in the purchasing power of money.

Conventional thinking says that you must be conservative with investments as you approach retirement, as well as during your retirement years. If you have enough money and if inflation is not a significant factor, you may get by with investing all your money in very conservative investments. However, most people need a portfolio with the growth potential of stocks and real estate in order to have the best chances of generating an income that keeps up with inflation. Too much exposure to more aggressive investments, however, exposes you to the risk of a market downturn, which, in turn, could put your retirement security at risk. Having a properly diversified portfolio matched to your risk tolerance is key to helping you outpace inflation and achieve your financial goals.

Retirement Income Strategies

Investing wisely for wealth accumulation is one thing, while converting those investments into a retirement income stream you cannot outlive is a completely different story. While much attention has been devoted to the accumulation phase of investing, insufficient attention is often devoted to the distribution phase.

As one enters retirement, their focus typically shifts from building wealth to managing and preserving it. A major challenge is to make an investment portfolio provide inflation adjusted cash flow for the remainder of a person's life — and through different economic and market conditions. Satisfying the desire for safety with your investments with the need for growth requires careful planning.

How Long Will Your Money Last?

Estimating how long your money will last is an important step in retirement planning. If you withdraw too much money from your investments each year, you risk running out of money. The chart on the following pages illustrates how long your money would last if you invested $1 million, took $50,000 annual withdrawals and earned annual investment returns ranging from 2% to 10%. The annual withdrawals are increased each year by 3½% to keep up with inflation and withdrawals are taxed each year at a rate of 20%.

		Annual Investment Return				
Years	Annual Distribution	2% Return	4% Return	6% Return	8% Return	10% Return
1	($50,000)	$1,000,000	$1,000,000	$1,000,000	$1,000,000	$1,000,000
2	($51,750)	$965,600	$981,200	$996,800	$1,012,400	$1,028,000
3	($53,561)	$928,886	$960,020	$991,654	$1,023,788	$1,056,420
4	($55,436)	$889,758	$936,323	$984,407	$1,034,035	$1,085,230
5	($57,376)	$848,115	$909,962	$974,892	$1,043,003	$1,114,395
6	($59,384)	$803,849	$880,787	$962,934	$1,050,543	$1,143,875
7	($61,463)	$756,852	$848,638	$948,345	$1,056,493	$1,173,626
8	($63,614)	$707,007	$813,348	$930,928	$1,060,679	$1,203,594
9	($65,840)	$654,196	$774,743	$910,472	$1,062,913	$1,233,724
10	($68,145)	$598,296	$732,641	$886,754	$1,062,992	$1,263,947
11	($70,530)	$539,179	$686,850	$859,538	$1,060,698	$1,294,192
12	($72,998)	$476,711	$637,171	$828,573	$1,055,796	$1,324,377
13	($75,553)	$410,756	$583,394	$793,594	$1,048,033	$1,354,408
14	($78,198)	$341,171	$525,301	$754,320	$1,037,136	$1,384,186
15	($80,935)	$267,806	$462,661	$710,452	$1,022,812	$1,413,595
16	($83,767)	$190,509	$395,237	$661,677	$1,004,747	$1,442,510
17	($86,699)	$109,119	$322,777	$607,660	$982,603	$1,470,793
18	($89,734)	$23,472	$245,019	$548,047	$956,016	$1,498,289
19	($92,874)	$0	$161,690	$482,466	$924,596	$1,524,829
20	($96,125)		$72,504	$410,521	$887,924	$1,550,226
21	($99,489)		$0	$331,794	$845,550	$1,574,274
22	($102,972)			$245,843	$796,992	$1,596,747
23	($106,576)			$152,200	$741,733	$1,617,396
24	($110,306)			$50,373	$679,218	$1,635,949
25	($114,166)			$0	$608,852	$1,652,107
26	($118,162)				$529,999	$1,665,543
27	($122,298)				$441,975	$1,675,897
28	($126,578)				$344,050	$1,682,779
29	($131,009)				$235,441	$1,685,760
30	($135,594)				$115,308	$1,684,372
31	($140,340)				$0	$1,678,104
32	($145,252)					$1,666,399
33	($150,335)					$1,648,649
34	($155,597)					$1,624,192
35	($161,043)					$1,592,307
36	($166,680)					$1,552,207

Years	Annual Distribution	Annual Investment Return				
		2% Return	4% Return	6% Return	8% Return	10% Return
37	($172,513)					$1,503,036
38	($178,551)					$1,443,865
39	($184,801)					$1,373,681
40	($191,269)					$1,291,383
41	($197,963)					$1,195,775
42	($204,892)					$1,085,555
43	($212,063)					$959,312
44	($219,485)					$815,512
45	($227,167)					$652,488
46	($235,118)					$468,433
47	($243,347)					$261,385
48	($251,864)					$29,215
49	($260,679)					$0
Total Distribution		1,158,721	1,390,361	1,773,392	2,560,846	5,796,763

Retirement Income Sources

Not all retirement income sources are the same. Some sources of retirement income are conservative and may provide safety of principal and stable, although lower, returns. Other investments are more aggressive but offer the potential for higher amounts of income should investment returns be positive. This doesn't mean one source of retirement income is better than another.

While many investors would like to invest only in conservative investments during retirement, most need growth investments to help them keep pace with inflation. Balancing the desire for safety with the need for growth is a delicate act.

More conservative, even "guaranteed", investments can provide a sense of security in knowing that in the event of an economic downturn, your income and principal have a good chance of remaining stable. The problem with these investments is they often have a low rate of return and may not provide a lifetime income that keeps up with inflation.

Investments that offer more growth potential, and more risk, may provide income that keeps pace with, or exceeds, inflation. One of the issues with these more aggressive investments is they are more volatile – their values fluctuate to a much greater degree than more conservative investments. In the event that investment values have dropped, but you still need to take a distribution for income purposes, you risk losing some of your principal.

Below are two common strategies for distributing retirement income from investment portfolios.

1. The Time-Segmented Bucket Strategy

The Time Segmented Bucket Strategy is a strategy that provides secure retirement income though conservative or guaranteed investments in the early years of retirement and segregates riskier investments for use years after retirement begins.

This strategy spreads a person's investments across multiple investment "buckets", each designated to produce income over a certain period of time. These "buckets" of money will hold different investments ranging from conservative to aggressive. The more aggressive the investment, the longer the time frame the investment is held.

Different numbers of "buckets" may be used with this strategy depending on how many investments you want to use and how segregated you want them to be. The amount of money allocated to each bucket is determined by performing an in-depth analysis of a person's goals, attitudes about investing and risk tolerance. In this example, we illustrate a strategy using two buckets.

How It Works

The first bucket is often funded with a conservative portfolio comprised mainly of less risky investments such as short-term, high credit quality bond funds. This "conservative bucket" will be the bucket that you make distributions from each month or quarter for living expenses. Bucket one will contain enough money to make distributions for five years.

Bucket two is funded with a more aggressive portfolio containing a higher percentage of equities. Every five years or so, you will refill bucket one from bucket two.

The psychology behind this strategy is that it may cause less anxiety for the investor by having stable investments to derive your income from during the short term, while allowing you to leave the more volatile assets (stock and real estate funds) untouched for a longer period of time. If you can mentally divide your investments into different buckets, understanding that the riskier investment buckets won't be used for many years, it can help combat the urge to sell the more volatile investments during negative performing years. Because the more volatile asset classes are segregated with the understanding that they will not be used for a period of many years, it helps you to be more mentally prepared for the volatility these investments will incur.

2. The Systematic Withdrawal Strategy

With the Systematic Withdrawal Strategy, a person takes withdrawals from a diversified portfolio of stock, bond and real estate funds. Distributions are made each month or quarter from the portfolio and the portfolio is rebalanced regularly to the target allocation. Unlike the Time Segmented Bucket Strategy, the Systematic Withdrawal Strategy does not segregate the different types of investments into different categories to be used at various times.

Alternative methods exist for taking systematic distributions. One method is to distribute equal amounts out of each investment fund based on its percentage allocation of the portfolio. For example, if you are taking $5,000 per month from a portfolio containing ten funds and each fund represents 10% of the portfolio, you would distribute 10% from each fund ($500) each month.

If you are using this method, it is important to work with a custodian and advisor that does not charge transaction fees for each trade you place; otherwise, the transaction costs you incur each month will greatly erode your investment return and negate the effectiveness of this method of distribution.

A second method requires you to deposit six to eighteen months of desired income into a money market fund. Your monthly income is distributed from this money market fund and the portfolio is periodically rebalanced to maintain the allocation to the money market fund.

Systematic Withdrawal Methods

There are two different types of systematic withdrawal methods: the Specified Dollar Amount and the Percent of Annual Portfolio Value.

The Specified Dollar Amount withdraws a fixed amount annually and adjusts that amount each year for inflation. This method can provide a stable income stream and preserve your living standard over time. The portfolio may only survive, however, if future withdrawals represent a small percentage of the portfolio's value.

The Percent of Annual Portfolio Value method withdraws a fixed percentage of money based on annual portfolio values. This method makes it unlikely that you will deplete retirement assets because a sudden drop in portfolio value would be accompanied by a proportional decrease in withdrawals. This method, however, can produce wide swings in your living standard when investment returns are volatile.

The 4% Rule

The "4% rule" is a common rule of thumb for providing sustainable retirement income. According to this rule, if you invest in a "moderate" portfolio containing approximately 60% equities and 40% fixed income, you can initially withdraw 4% from your portfolio (including dividends and interest), increase your withdrawal amount each year for inflation, and still have a very high probability of not running out of money over a 30-year retirement. [33]

A concern with this strategy is severely depleting the account during sustained periods of negative returns such as during 2008 and 2009. During these severe market downturns, it is advised you reduce distributions if possible and take money for living expenses from only the bond funds in the portfolio or from a money market account, giving the equities a chance to rebound. Once the equities have rebounded, regular distributions from each asset class may begin again.

Summary

Today's retirees face many challenges. These include increasing life expectancies, volatile stock markets, soaring healthcare costs, the uncertainty of Social Security, rising taxes, inflation and more. Figuring out how to make our money last for a retirement that could range from 20 to 40 years, while the price of almost everything we buy increases and taxes continue to rise, can be a real dilemma. Unless one has a very large sum of money and can live comfortably on the income off of safe investments alone, it is usually necessary to own some growth investments to provide an income that lasts many years and outpaces inflation.

Every type of investment carries a certain type of risk and while nobody likes to see his or her investments decline in value, nobody likes the thought of running out of money or facing an ever-decreasing standard of living. Developing an efficient strategy for distributing income from your investments can help ensure your money keeps up with inflation and lasts as long as you do.

Financial Strategies For Selling A Farm Or Ranch

Conclusion

You have worked hard to create the value in your farm or ranch. When you go to sell your property, you need to work smart to preserve that value and make your money work for you.

Selling a highly appreciated farm or ranch creates significant tax consequences and important retirement and estate planning considerations. The amount of tax you will owe on a sale and the income you are able to generate from the proceeds are largely dependent on how proactive you are at engaging in financial planning prior to a sale.

Whether you are investing in real estate or the stock and bond market, it is wise to work with professionals. The right advisors can help you select the right investments and manage those assets, freeing you to enjoy your retirement years.

Proper planning for the sale of your property should address all areas of your family's financial needs and involve a collaborative effort among tax, investment and legal professionals. Your advisors should be experienced in working with the financial tools and investment products discussed in this book.

About The Author
Chris Nolt

President
Solid Rock Wealth Management, Inc.
Solid Rock Realty Advisors, LLC.

Chris Nolt is President of Solid Rock Wealth Management, Inc. and Solid Rock Realty Advisors, LLC, sister companies dedicated to helping agricultural families throughout the country save taxes on the sale of their farm or ranch and plan for retirement.

Chris grew up in Lewistown, Montana. Working on large cattle ranches every summer throughout his high school and college days, Chris gained a deep respect for the work ethic and character of the agricultural family. Having seen the effects from a lack of good financial planning among the agricultural community, Chris determined to help farm and ranch families make smart decisions with their money.

After graduating with a degree in business from Montana State University, Chris entered the financial services business in 1989. Since then, he has been helping people reduce taxes, protect and preserve their assets and invest wisely. Chris' educational articles have been featured in numerous farm and ranch publications and he has presented educational seminars for agricultural families, CPAs, attorneys and ranch brokers in several states. A father of two children, an avid outdoorsman and devoted Christian, Chris lives in Bozeman, Montana and Fountain Hills, Arizona.

To speak with Chris about planning for the sale of your farm or ranch, call 406-582-1264.

This material was created to provide accurate and reliable information on the subjects covered. It is not, however, intended to provide specific legal, tax or other professional advice. Readers should seek the advice of their own tax and legal advisors. Tax information provided can be sourced at www.irs.gov and your state's revenue department website. Because individuals' situations and objectives vary, this information is not intended to indicate suitability for any particular individual. IRC Section 1031 and IRC Section 664 Charitable Remainder Trust are complex tax codes. The services of an appropriate tax or legal professional should be sought regarding your individual situation. Diversification neither assures a profit nor guarantees against loss in a declining market. Past performance does not guarantee future results. All investing is subject to risk, including possible loss of principal. There is no guarantee that any particular asset allocation or mix of funds will meet your investment objectives or provide you with a given level of income. The performance of an index is not an exact representation of any particular investment, as you cannot invest directly in an index.

Sources

1. CD performance is based on average historical interest rates from Bloomberg. Data prior to 2013 is from Lipper.

2. AdvisoryWorld and Lipper

3. The Vanguard Group, as of December 31, 2015

4. THE JOURNAL OF FINANCE • VOL. LXIII, NO. 4 • AUGUST 2008

5. Barras, Laurent, Scaillet, Wermers, and Russ, "False Discoveries in Mutual Fund Performance: Measuring Luck in Estimated Alphas" (May 2008). Robert H. Smith School Research Paper No. RHS 06-043 Available at SSRN: http://ssrn.com/abstract=869748

6. Mutual Fund Landscape, Dimensional Fund Advisors 2015. US-domiciled mutual fund data is from the CRSP Survivor-Bias-Free US Mutual Fund Database, provided by the Center for Research in Security Prices, University of Chicago.

7. Bloomberg, London Share Price Database, and Centre for Research in Finance

8. www.morningstar.com/cover/videocenter.aspx?id=650699

9. Performance data for January 1970–August 2008 provided by CRSP; performance data for September 2008–December 2015 provided by Bloomberg. S&P data provided by Standard & Poor's Index Services Group. US bonds and bills data © Stocks, Bonds, Bills, and Inflation Yearbook™, Ibbotson Associates,

Chicago (annually updated work by Roger G. Ibbotson and Rex A. Sinquefield).

10. Yahoo Finance 1/7/14

11. Gary P. Brinson, Brian D. Singer, and Gilbert L. Beebower Financial Analysts Journal, May/June 1991,

12. The Vanguard Group, 2013.

13. Morningstar Direct 2015.

14. Data from Standard & Poors, MSCI, Barclay's Capital, Google Finance, and Dow Jones

15. Dimensional Fund Advisors, www.dfaus.com

16. MSCI

17. Morningstar Direct 2015

18. Morningstar Direct 2014.

19. Dimensional Fund Advisors, www.dfaus.com

20. Dimensional Fund Advisors, www.dfaus.com

21. www.vanguard.com/pdf/icrpr.pdf

22. 2014 DALBAR QAIB Study

23. Morningstar® EnCorr®; FMRCo, as of 12/31/2015.

24. www.forbes.com/sites/rogeraitken/2015/01/21/why-invest-in-hedge-funds-if-they-dont-outperform-the-market/#2690559e1f56

25. www.hedgefundresearch.com

26. www.kauffman.org

27. Siegel, Jeremy. Future for Investors 2005 with updates to 2013. (2) ." Warren Buffett, Why Stocks Beat Gold and Bonds, Fortune, February 9, 2012.

28. Mouton & Co. Inc. Individual Mortality Rates, 2004

29. EBRI.org. Notes, October 2014. What is the Distribution of Lifetime Health Care Costs From Age 65? By Anthony Webb and Natalia A. Zhivan. March 2010.

30. 2014 Medicare & You, National Medicare Handbook, Centers for Medicare and Medicaid Services, September 2013

31. Genworth 2014 Cost of Care Survey

32. The 2012 Long-Term Projections for Social Security. www.cbo.gov

33. Cooley, Hubbard, and Walz, Retirement Savings: Choosing a Withdrawal Rate That Is Sustainable," 16–21.

Made in the USA
San Bernardino, CA
07 June 2017